THE REGULATION OF THE CONSUMER FINANCE INDUSTRY:

A Case Study of Rate Ceilings and Loan Limits in New York State

MICHAEL KAWAJA

Studies in Consumer Credit, No. 3
GRADUATE SCHOOL OF BUSINESS,
COLUMBIA UNIVERSITY
DISTRIBUTED BY
COLUMBIA UNIVERSITY PRESS

Printed in the United States of America

TO CARL

Contents

Tables

Charts

Appendixes

Foreword

The consumer finance industry comprises the cash loan operations of finance companies that are regulated by special state statutes. In 1964, the industry supplied $8.3 billion in loans to consumers, including $0.5 billion in loans to consumers in New York State. The industry operates under regulations that typically place ceilings on the rates lenders may charge and limits on the sizes of loans they may make. The exact levels of these rate ceilings and loan limits vary from state to state but their general objectives are the same.

This is a case study of the rate ceilings and loan limits in New York State. New York was chosen for detailed analysis because more comprehensive data are available for New York than for most other states. Also, as will be shown, the New York rate ceilings and loan limits are lower and hence more restrictive than the rate ceilings and loan limits in most other states. Their effects are thus more perceptible.

This study seeks to answer two basic types of questions: How did the rate and loan size regulations in the consumer finance industry evolve? What are their effects on the character of the lending service provided, the volume of lending facilities that are supplied under regulation, and the earnings rates of lenders? The study is designed to develop answers to these questions in a manner that will be useful in several ways.

First, there currently exists no up-to-date and integrated analysis of the economic, political, and legal factors that shaped the development of the consumer finance industry's regulation; this study strives to remedy this and in the process to clarify the objectives of the industry's regulation.

Second, the study demonstrates the effects of more or less restrictive ceilings on rates and maximum limits on loan sizes. It thus provides a basis for evaluating the adequacy of any particular regulatory pattern if rate ceilings and loan limits are to be perpetuated. This may be done by comparing the actual effects of rate ceilings and loan limits, which are studied here, with their desired effects.

Third, the continuing controversy in the economic literature over the desirability of more or less regulation has generated surprisingly few empirical studies of the actual effects of regulation. In this connection, this study is designed to be of use to researchers who are interested in the economics of regulation generally. Market adjustments to regulation are dealt with in detail. In New York and most other states with which comparisons are made, revisions of the consumer finance industry's rate structures are infrequent, and basic market conditions change constantly and rapidly. Thus a substantial range of experience with a given regulatory structure is accumulated. This makes the consumer finance industry a particularly good vehicle for illustrating some of the less obvious effects of regulation.

Finally, this is a most opportune time for airing the effects of regulating the consumer finance industry. The National Conference of Commissioners on Uniform State Laws has drafted a model bill for regulating consumer credit. It is widely believed that this model legislation will shape the future course of the industry's regulation. Among the issues being faced by the Conference, of prime interest is the question whether there should be rate ceilings and loan limits, and, if so, just what are the effects of more or less restrictive rate ceilings and loan limits. It is just these kinds of questions that are dealt with in this study.

This monograph grew out of my doctoral dissertation, which was completed at Columbia University in 1964. I am indebted to the members of my dissertation committee and others who guided me in completing the dissertation. I am also indebted to numerous individuals who supplied helpful comments for modifying and supplementing the dissertation for publication in its current form. My greatest debt is to Robert P. Shay, Professor of Banking and Finance at Columbia University, who assisted me with my dissertation and who first suggested the idea of this monograph, and painstakingly reviewed its many preliminary drafts.

I am also much indebted to John Chapman, Professor Emeritus of Banking, Columbia University, who made this monograph possible from funds provided by the Alumni of the Consumer Credit Management Program; and to Richard O. Wiesner of the New York State Consumer Finance Association whose comments were helpful at every stage of the project. For constructive suggestions on one or other aspects of this study, at one or another of its stages, I am thankful to

Roger F. Murray, formerly of Columbia University and now of Teachers Insurance and Annuity Association; Gordon Shillinglaw, Professor of Accounting, Columbia University; Clarence Huizenga, Lecturer, University of California, Los Angeles; and my research assistants, Richard Carter and Melvyn Masuda, who assisted in carrying out many of the statistical computations. It is also a pleasure to acknowledge the assistance of Charles H. Gushee, President of Financial Publishing Company, who supplied the average legal rates in Appendix B which provide the basis for significant portions of the analysis. Finally, I am grateful for the research and typing assistance provided by the Bureau of Business and Economic Research, UCLA, and for the use of the computer facilities of the Western Data Processing Center, also at UCLA. Virginia Meltzer edited the manuscript and H. Irving Forman drew the charts.

I am fully and solely responsible for any errors which remain in the paper.

Michael Kawaja
Los Angeles, California

CHAPTER 1
Summary

The consumer finance industry as it exists in New York[1] and 48 other states has its origins in legislation which was first enacted in the early 1900's to combat loan sharking in the highest cost necessitous loan market.

The specific levels of the original ceilings on the industry's charges were established by trial and error testing of the efficacy of alternative ceilings in combatting loan sharking. They were a compromise between the demands of philanthropic organizations for lower rates and those of representatives of the small loan industry for higher rates. Also, to obtain legislative sanction, these rate ceilings had to gain the approval of a public which had previously believed that "6 per cent" was a reasonable maximum charge to meet the needs of legal lenders to make a profit.

The limits placed on the industry's loan sizes (here called "loan limits") were determined by the intent of the laws to protect the necessitous borrower who typically made small loans. In addition, in the early 1900's, when the industry was initiated, some loan limit had to be set to meet constitutional requirements. Specifically, the Supreme Courts of a number of states had declared unconstitutional laws which had been intended to combat loan sharking but which placed no limits on loan sizes.

Criteria for Evaluating Regulation

The principal bases on which the adequacy of rate ceilings and loan limits are judged in New York are: (1) the characteristics of the loans

[1] "New York" refers to New York State throughout the paper.

that are made (e.g., their sizes and prices), (2) the amount of credit made available (here referred to as the amount of lending facilities), and (3) the earnings rates of licensees.

In light of the objectives of regulation, the criteria used in New York to evaluate rate ceilings and loan limits are appropriate. That is to say, whether rate ceilings and loan limits are adequate should depend upon: (1) whether lenders are making the kinds of loans to the classes of borrowers contemplated by the statute; (2) whether adequate amounts of lending facilities are being made available; and (3) whether rates on loans are as low as possible, consistent with ensuring that the desired type and amount of credit is generated. However, the third criterion – earnings rates – has to be qualified.

If competition is effective, it will force adjustment of the characteristics and volume of the credit service. This adjustment will continue until lenders achieve no more than fair earnings rates. The level of earnings rates will then not vary with the rate structure and earnings will not be a useful criterion for evaluating the rate structure. In fact, under these conditions, changing the rate structure will have no impact on earnings rates, at least after a reasonable time lag to allow the industry to adjust. It will affect only the characteristics and volume of the credit service. However, in the absence of strong competitive pressures, earnings rates may vary with the rate structure. That is to say, if competition is ineffective then, under some rate structures, lenders may achieve rates of earnings higher than required to ensure that they will supply the desired types and amounts of credit. Rate structure reductions may, under these conditions, reduce earnings rates without affecting the characteristics or volume of the credit service. (For example, under these conditions rate reductions may reduce earnings rates without causing a contraction of loan volume).

To sum up, in order to ascertain whether earnings rates are a useful criterion to evaluate the rate structure, it is necessary to examine whether adjustments to changes in the rate structure (such as changes in the sizes of loans) actually occur. It is also necessary to ascertain whether lenders earn more or less under different rate structures. Chapters 5-7 deal with the effects of regulation in New York and show the extent to which the industry in that state adjusts to its rate structure; they will now be summarized. First, however, it will be helpful to put the New York regulations in perspective by reviewing the national pattern of regulation.

The National Pattern of Regulation

The New York loan limit was $800 in 1964. This was low compared to the loan limits (which range from $300 to $5,000) in most other states. In New York and virtually all other states, the rate ceiling is graduated with the size of the loan so that the larger the loan in a particular state, the lower the permitted rate.

There is an inverse correlation between average rates charged and loan limits *among different states*. This makes it difficult, or in some cases impossible, to distinguish between the effects of rate ceilings and those of loan limits (since the effects of rate ceilings were examined in part through an analysis of actual average rates in different states and since these average rates do not vary independent of loan limits).

Rate structure adjustments are infrequent in New York (and most other states). They occur on the average roughly once in ten years. These adjustments normally take the form of loan limit increases. Rate ceiling changes alone have been rare, although new rates must of course be enacted to cover the new loan sizes permitted.

Regulation and the Characteristics of Loans and Borrowers

LOAN CHARACTERISTICS

Loan limits, rate ceilings, price levels, and per capita real incomes determine the sizes of loans which are made by the consumer finance industry in New York. Low loan limits in New York, as in other states, tend to lead to small average loan sizes. However, this effect of the loan limits may be at least partially offset, as it is in New York, by relatively low rate ceilings on small loan sizes. These relatively low rates on small loans encourage lenders to make larger loans within the permitted range of loan sizes.

If a loan limit is to permit consumer finance companies to continue to serve the same class of borrowers over time and to meet the demand for loans of a given purpose, it must be adjusted at short intervals. (The reason is that price levels and per capita income change constantly.) This practice is not followed in New York nor in most other states. The result is that there is a gradual erosion of the purchasing power of the loan limit as price levels increase, and the adequacy of the loan limit in terms of consumers' per capita real incomes declines throughout the period the loan limit is in force.

In New York, there has been a long-term down trend in average rates charged associated with increases in average loan sizes which result at least in part from rising prices and incomes. Barring rate ceiling increases, the only way in which this average rate decline can be halted is to periodically adjust the range of *each* loan size bracket, and not merely the highest loan bracket as is generally done in New York. In this way, lenders will be encouraged to make loans over the full range of permitted sizes, and will not concentrate, as they now do in New York, only on relatively large loans.

BORROWER CHARACTERISTICS

On the average, lenders assume less risk (as measured by the ratio of reserve for bad debts to the dollar value of loans outstanding) in their credit extensions in states with relatively low average rates. It was not possible to ascertain whether this is due to the lower rate alone or to the higher loan limits which are typically associated with lower average rates. These higher loan limits make it possible for lenders to make larger, less risky loans. In New York, however, the average risk of customers served is relatively low. This is probably due mostly to the low average rate charged in New York since New York has a relatively low loan limit which, if it were dominant, would have resulted in the average risk in New York being high.

Regulation and the Amount of Lending Facilities

There are relatively few lenders in New York and most other relatively low rate states. Also, there are relatively few loan branches in New York. The large average sizes of lenders and branch offices in New York appear to be due mainly to New York's low rate. This weeds out all but the very low cost lenders and loan branches (which are typically the larger lenders and larger loan branches).

Low rates tend to lead to few loans being made. But this effect of low rates may be offset by the opposing effect of loan limits. (Paradoxically, the number of loans is typically higher in states which have low loan limits. This is probably due to "doubling up," the practice of borrowing from several sources when the loan limit is restrictive.) However, New York has relatively few loans in proportion to its population in spite of its low loan limit. This suggests that New York's low rate is the dominant determinant of the number of loans made by

New York's consumer finance industry.

Low rates would be expected to lead to a relatively small dollar volume of loans being made. However, low average rates are typically associated with high loan limits. The high loan limits tend to lead to a relatively large dollar volume of loans being made in spite of the relatively low rates. New York has a low average rate and a low loan limit and these reinforce each other to result in a relatively small dollar volume of loans being made in New York, relative to the state's population.

The relatively small number and dollar volume of loans made under the New York statute indicates that it attracts and can support only relatively few lenders or loan branches, as observed earlier. This effect is reinforced by the necessity for lenders and branch offices to be large to achieve the low average cost operation required to survive under New York's low rate.

Regulation and Earnings

Compared to other states, New York has a very low average gross income rate but not a correspondingly low average net earnings rate. The relationship between gross and net income among all states (including New York) was examined to determine whether this pattern found in New York was typical. However, there was found to be no systematic relationship between gross earnings rates and net earnings rates among states. This lack of correlation between gross and net earnings rates is explainable by cost differences among high and low rate states. States with high average gross income tend to have high costs and states with low average gross income tend to have low costs. The differences in costs among high and low rate states results from adjustments of loan sizes, risk, and the structure of the consumer finance industry, to the level of rates. In other words, the nature of loan services in a given state is largely determined by the average gross income of that state.

These adjustments in loan service are evident in the New York consumer finance industry. In 1964, the New York industry had relatively low average gross income associated with low average operating costs. It was also characterized by relatively (1) large average loan size, within the loan ceiling, (2) low average risk due to the high selectivity of customers served, and (3) few but large lenders and branch offices.

An analysis of trends in the New York industry over the 1936-65 period show that, in response to a steadily and rapidly declining average gross income, average operating costs (as a percentage of average loans outstanding) in New York have fallen quite steadily. However, this did not prevent a slight decline in net earnings. The cost reductions associated with the average gross income decline appear to result from three sources. These are (1) increases in the average size of loans made, (2) a reduction in the average risk of borrowers accommodated, and (3) a growth in the average size of lenders and loan branches.

It should be recognized that since loan limits are correlated with average gross rates among states, there is a lack of correlation between loan limits and net earnings. This is a corollary of the lack of systematic relationship between gross and net earnings. The lack of correlation between the rate structure (i.e., both rates and loan limits) and net earnings results from the industry's adjustment to the gross income attainable under its given rate structure. But this does not mean that one should be indifferent to alternative rate structures.

The central finding of this study is that the characteristics of the consumer finance industry differ when average rates are low and when average rates are high. If the public interest requires that credit be made available legally to the high risk borrower then preference should be given to a rate structure which yields a relatively high average gross rate. Similarly, one who prefers to have a relatively large dollar volume of loans supplied will prefer a high average rate to a low one; and one who seeks to perpetuate a high proportion of small independent operators, as opposed to large chains, will similarly prefer a rate structure which will yield a high average gross rate, and so on.

But the desire to avoid the possibility of excessive average earnings rates in a state should not be the basis, as it is in New York, for altering the rate structure to ensure that it yields a low average gross rate. The industry, as it does in New York, will adjust the loan services it provides to its rate structure so that net earnings will not decline with gross rate.

CHAPTER 2

A Historical Perspective

This chapter traces the historical development of the Uniform Small Loan Law, which served as the model for the law that regulates the consumer finance industry in New York state.

Early Attitudes Toward Credit

THE CREDIT PRACTICES OF EARLY HISTORY

Loans were probably made even in the most primitive societies of prehistoric times. By custom, tribesmen in those societies shared their wealth[1] and there was probably no distinction between loans on the basis of their purpose. Credit was treated simply as charitable aid regardless of whether or not it was to be used for productive or consumptive purposes.

The antipathy to credit charges probably has its origin in these tribal lending practices. Because loans were expected and customary charity, there was no justifiable basis for charging for them. However, as civilization advanced, capital became an important element in economic life, and credit for productive purposes (originally these were mostly loans of seeds and animals) grew in importance. There was often a charge for these loans, but this took the form of sharing the "fruit of the loan." Still, as a rule loans for consumptive purposes were free. But it is believed that confusion between the two types of credits resulted in charges sometimes being made on nonproductive as well as on productive loans.[2]

[1] Cliffe, Leslie, *Essays*, 2nd edition, Boston, Harvard University Press, 1948, p. 244.

[2] Sidney Homer, *A History of Interest Rates*, New Brunswick, N. J., 1963, p. 18.

The earliest recorded credit customs are found in the Babylonian Code of Hammurabi, circa 2,000 B.C. Hammurabi merely recognized the customary charges of the earlier (Sumerian) period and established them as legal maxima. These lasted about 1,200 years.[3]

The Greeks later adopted Babylonian banking methods, but permitted them to operate in an atmosphere of virtually complete laissez-faire. In turn, they passed on their credit practices to the Romans – Roman bankers were mostly Greeks. The Romans in turn adapted these credit practices to their authoritarian society and, under the Justinian Code, established a series of rate maxima that became models for other countries.[4]

CREDIT PRACTICES IN MEDIEVAL EUROPE

Most of the medieval European credit practices are traceable to Roman law and custom, although the Christian tradition was also a dominant influence. The Christian tradition in turn was based largely on Hebrew religious laws. These laws prohibited charging for loans. This edict is explainable at least in part by the fact that the Israelites led an isolated existence (not unlike that of the primitive tribes of prehistoric times) and made loans only as accommodations to each other.

Like the forms of credit, the medieval exceptions to the prohibition against credit charges were based on both Roman custom and Roman law. In general, compensation for loss incurred in making a loan was regarded as a licit exception to the prohibition. One type of financial contract, termed *damnum emergens* by the Romans who developed it, found particular favor in Western Europe. It was compensation for loss resulting from the borrower's failure to repay. However, direct loss was often hard to prove. Accordingly, an alternative contract form, termed *lucrum cessans,* was often used. *Lucrum cessans* is a probable loss suffered by a lender in foregoing the profit he might have been able to make with his money if he had not lent it out.

While *damnum emergens* and *lucrum cessans* were the main exceptions to the general prohibition against charging for credit, there were others. As they multiplied, they whittled away the blanket prohibition against credit charges. As this occurred, the term "interest" began to be used to refer to the widening category of permitted

[3] *Ibid.,* p. 26.
[4] *Ibid.,* pp. 32-43.

charges. "Usury," which had hitherto applied to any credit charge, was now restricted only to those charges that were not generally approved. That is to say, usury referred only to charges other than or beyond "interest".[5]

Before the end of the medieval period proper, the opportunity for capital investment had become widespread. The scholastics argued that, under these conditions, a lender usually suffered a loss (by foregoing profit). He was thus almost always entitled to the compensation permitted under *lucrum cessans*. The *Triple Contract* defined the class of transactions under which these conditions prevailed. Its acceptance marked the final turning point in the traditional Catholic attitude toward credit. In the eighteenth century, the church accepted more forms of credit charges and, finally, in the early 1800's decreed that all charges allowed by law were permissible.[6]

In the fifteenth century, more than two hundred years before the Catholic clergy had approved the Triple Contract, leading Protestant reformers, most notably Martin Luther and John Calvin, had begun to develop their own theories of usury. Luther took the position that a Christian was under no obligation to observe the Mosaic Code. Calvin recognized the need for credit charges and argued that the canonists had misinterpreted the Scriptures. The only rule governing credit transactions under his interpretation was that they should not injure the borrower.

The expression of doubts about the traditional and biblical teachings on usury by such prominent religious leaders as Luther and Calvin encouraged commercial interests which moved to gain legal acceptance of a more permissive view toward credit. They were so effective that by the seventeenth century the question in England and other Protestant countries was no longer whether charges were permissible, but what were the economic effects of different ceilings on these charges.

The separation of England from the authority of the Roman Church cleared the way for a formal recognition of the practice of charging for credit. And, in 1545, the practice was legalized by the Statute of Henry VIII. This statute went through repeal and re-enactment until

[5] Homer estimates this change took place around 1200 A.D., *ibid.*, p. 73. "Interest" is itself derived from the Latin *interesse*. Its earliest usage was to refer to money which under Roman law was due from a debtor who had defaulted. See Maurice A. Unger, "Profit, Usury, and Law," *American Business Law Journal*, Vol. II, No. 1, January 1964, p. 13.

[6] Homer, *op. cit.*, p. 81.

1713 when the Statute of Anne fixed a maximum charge of five per cent on all loans.[7] The Statute of Anne remained in force in England for a period of one hundred and forty years. It was the model followed by the American colonies.[8] The American usury laws differed from state to state but generally permitted higher charges than the five per cent per year allowed in England. Presumably, this was so that they would attract capital for investment in the colonies.[9]

SUMMARY

This fleeting historical survey reveals two important points. First, the antipathy to credit charges is long entrenched in our culture. It has been passed on from earliest recorded societies, and appears to have grown out of the organization of these societies. It has been reinforced by religious teachings and tradition. Second, the credit charges and practices which gained acceptance did so as exceptions to the basic rule that credit should be free. It was the multiplication, adaptation, and broadening of these exceptions that broke down the rule that credit should be free.

The Loan Shark Era

This brings us to the beginning of what is now referred to as the "loan shark" era, the period from around 1880 to 1920. There were many circumstances that gave rise to dominance of the consumer loan field by loan sharks during this period. America was completing its transition from a rural nation of largely self-sustaining producers to an economy based on mass production. The percentage of wage earners in the population was increasing. And, whereas before individuals had produced for their own consumption, specialization now made them dependent on their wages.

By present day criteria, the wage earner's standard of living was low. The margin between his earnings and his expenditures on the bare necessities required for survival was narrow. Thus, whenever his flow of income was interrupted he had no choice but to beg or borrow. However, there was no organized supply of loans to meet his demand. Commercial banks had traditionally extended loans only to business,

[7] Franklin W. Ryan, *Usury and Usury Laws*, New York, 1924, p. 13.
[8] *Loc. cit.*
[9] See Louis N. Robinson and Rolf Nugent, *Regulation of the Small Loan Business*, New York, 1935, p. 28.

and they had not yet entered the consumer lending field. Loan sharks stepped into the breach and typically charged rates that were many times (in some cases a hundred or more times) higher than the usury ceilings.[10]

This practice is explained by the economic conditions of the time. First, in the late 1800's and early 1900's, there was a severe stigma attached to consumer borrowing.[11] Thus, typically, consumers borrowed only when "necessary." [12] In general the loans they demanded were too small and the risk was too great for them to be supplied profitably at rates permitted under the usury laws.[13] Lenders thus had to operate illegally if they were to engage profitably in a consumer cash loan business at all. They demanded compensation for this risk and for the social opprobrium attached to their illegal business. Further, they typically operated with their own funds, as the small loan business had not yet gained the respectability required for funds to be raised from the public. There was thus a shortage of capital at rates that would have yielded lenders compensation for the costs of conducting an illegal business.[14] Rates rose in response to these pressures.

Second, demand conditions were ripe for lenders to get the relatively high rates they asked. The stigma attached to consumer borrowing, the urgency that typically characterized the borrower's demand, and the borrower's fear of having the transaction exposed (since this often led to the loss of his employment)[15] minimized rate shopping.

Third, in their attempts to pass off their charges as being legal, the loan sharks devised various ways of disguising their true rates. In particular, they charged special collection and other fees that were ex-

[10] See William Hays Simpson, "Costs of Loans to Borrowers Under Unregulated Lending," *Law and Contemporary Problems*, Vol. VIII, 1941, pp. 73-77.

[11] See Wallace Mors, "Rate Regulation in the Field of Consumer Credit," Parts I and II, *Journal of Business*, January and April 1943), pp. 51-63, pp. 124-137.

[12] See, e.g., the detailed breakdown of the purposes of consumer cash loans made in 1914, in Reginald Heber Smith, *The Facts About the Small Loan Business and the Scientific Rate of Return*, Pennsylvania, 1922, pp. 4-5.

[13] See Clarence W. Wassam, *The Salary Loan Business in New York City*, New York, 1908, and Arthur H. Ham, *The Chattel Loan Business*, New York, 1909. For support of the position that the costs of making consumer loans as a percentage of the amount of the loan declines significantly as the loan increases in size, see Paul F. Smith, *Cost of Providing Consumer Credit*, New York, National Bureau of Economic Research, 1962, pp. 7-8.

[14] See Arthur Ham, "Remedial Loans — A Constructive Program," *Proceedings of the Academy of Political Science in the City of New York*, Vol. II, 1912, p. 162.

[15] See Robinson and Nugent, *op. cit.*, p. 68.

cluded from the quoted rate.[16] This rendered largely ineffective whatever little rate-shopping borrowers did. Since violation of the usury laws did not result in severe penalties, there was little deterrent to this kind of practice.[17]

In summary, therefore, in the loan shark era the cost of supplying consumer loans far exceeded the usury ceilings. The high degree of borrowers' insensitivity to the over-all level of rate charges and to the differences in charges among high-rate lenders created a monopoly for these lenders. Many of these lenders exploited this market power to earn excessive profits.[18] Further, by driving the consumer loan business underground, there was no doubt that the usury ceilings worsened borrowing conditions.

LEGISLATION IN THE LOAN SHARK ERA

Throughout the loan shark era, the consumer loan business was constantly brought to the attention of the public as case after case of loan shark activity was exposed. In an attempt to solve the problem, legislation of one sort or another was passed in a number of states. Most important, for the first time specific analysis of the problem was undertaken.[19] As a result several noteworthy constructive events emerged from this period. These included the establishment of philanthropic and semiphilanthropic loan agencies, the development of interest by the Russell Sage Foundation in the furthering of consumer loan legislation, and the beginning of experimentation with a profit-making small loan business.

The Philanthropic Approach. The philanthropic loan funds' charges, when there were any, failed to maintain the fund since they bore little or no relation to the cost of lending.[20] Prime among this kind of agency were those set up by employers. The employers had found that their employees often suffered such a loss in morale by getting deeply into debt that their efficiency became seriously impaired. Other philanthropic agencies were maintained by churches, fraternal lodges, and

[16] See Simpson, *op. cit.*, p. 75.

[17] See David J. Gallert, Walter S. Hilborn, and Geoffrey May, *Small Loan Legislation*, New York, 1932, pp. 48-51.

[18] See Wassam, *op. cit.*, p. 17.

[19] While Jeremy Bentham and others had dealt with the economics of legal ceilings on loan charges in general, they had evaded the problem of how to control loan sharking, granted the noncompetitive conditions.

[20] For example, the Hebrew Free Loan Society established in New York City in 1896 made small loans without any charge whatever. See Gallert, Hilborn, and May, *op. cit.*, p. 25.

individuals and groups of citizens organized for the express purpose of working for the general social benefit. The semiphilanthropic loan funds made charges at cost plus a limited return to the suppliers of capital.[21]

The philanthropic and semiphilanthropic remedial agencies proved unable to meet the growing demand for loans. Their chief lasting significance was that they marked the beginning of a new approach to the problem of combating the loan shark. Exposures, denunciations, and repressive legislation had proved ineffective. The new approach consisted of experimenting with actually making loans. In this way much of the experience was gained (e.g., relating to the effects of different charges) that later students used to formulate solutions to the loan shark problem within a framework of rate ceilings.

The Russell Sage Foundation. In 1908, the Russell Sage Foundation first entered into active promotion of consumer loan legislation. Russell Sage was a philanthropic organization, incorporated by a special act of the New York legislature in April 1907. Its entry into consumer loan legislative effort came about as a result of several factors. Among the most important of these factors were the Foundation's publication of Wassam's *The Salary Loan Business*[22] and Ham's *The Chattel Loan Business*[23] in 1908 and 1909, respectively. For about the next twenty years, the Foundation took the lead in analyzing the loan shark problem and drafting legislation designed to solve it.

Russell Sage played a part in testing the philanthropic approach and other attempts to solve the loan shark problem (e.g., promoting remedial loan companies and cooperative societies). However, its efforts were finally directed at obtaining legislation that would make possible a regulated profit-making small loan business. Both Wassam and Ham had concluded that this was the most promising line of attack on the loan shark.

[21] For example, the Provident Loan Society of New York incorporated in 1894 and the Workingmen's Loan Association incorporated in Rhode Island in 1895. The charter of the former provided that "No member or trustee . . . shall receive any compensation for his services, or any profit other than lawful interest on money loaned to it." The act of incorporation of the latter allowed a maximum rate of charge not exceeding one per cent a month.

[22] Wassam, *loc. cit.*

[23] Ham, *op. cit.* The Russell Sage Foundation had supplied funds for fellowships for special studies on social problems under the auspices of the New York School of Philanthropy. Fellowships were granted to Wassam and Ham who chose freely, from a wide range of possible topics, to study the consumer loan business (see Robinson and Nugent, *op. cit.*, p. 86).

A Regulated Profit-Making Small Loan Business. By the early 1900's, experimentation with a regulated profit-making consumer loan business was already underway in a number of states. Various rate limits were being tried and an attempt was being made to plug loopholes in the statutes as experience proved necessary. As a result of this trial and error procedure the Uniform Small Loan Law was drawn up in 1916. Variants of this law created consumer finance companies as they now exist and still provide the bases of the laws that govern the consumer finance industries in each of the states.

The Uniform Small Loan Law

In 1916, representatives of the Russell Sage Foundation, the American Association of Small Loan Brokers,[24] and the National Federation of Remedial Loan Associations met to draft a model consumer loan law for legislative guidance. The bill, the Uniform Small Loan Law, agreed upon at this meeting, met all the requirements that Russell Sage had found necessary in its trial and error legislative efforts in the various states. Its most important provisions are enumerated below.

1. A "small loan" was classified as a sum not exceeding $300. The purpose of the law as expressed in its first section was to render the business of making these small loans attractive to legitimate lenders. It intended thereby to protect borrowers against abusive and coercive practices of lenders. Experiments with various loan size limits had indicated that $300 demarcated the prime area of loan shark activity.

Further, decisions of the Supreme Courts of Pennsylvania and Illinois had held unconstitutional laws that had been intended to combat loan sharking but that had placed no limit on the amount of the loan. However, a subsequent decision of the Pennsylvania court supported the constitutionality of a law that was limited to loans of $300 and that permitted higher charges than allowed under the general usury law of that state. The laws of Massachusetts, Michigan, and New Jersey had set loan ceilings of $300. These precedents practically established that loans under $300 constituted a proper classification of small loan legislation.[25]

[24] Small Loan Brokers were lenders operating under the laws (existing in some states) that permitted profitable small loan operations.

[25] See Gallert, Hilborn, and May, *op. cit.*, p. 131. The constitutionality of exempting loans under $300 from the general usury laws lay in its interpretation as a proper exercise of the police power of the state.

2. A maximum charge of 3½ per cent per month on the unpaid balance was established on loans up to $300. This rate was all-inclusive, and no other charge was allowed. In providing this maximum, the Uniform Small Loan Law was a compromise between the views of the commercial lenders on the one hand and those of the Department of Remedial Loans of the Russell Sage Foundation and the National Federation of Remedial Loans on the other.[26]

Rates of 1, 1½, 2½, 3, 3½, and 4 per cent per month had been tried.[27] It had become clear that a rate of about 3 or 4 per cent a month was needed to attract legitimate capital into the business in sufficient quantities to drive out the loan sharks.

A rate limit of 3 per cent a month was first considered. But some lenders at the meeting argued that this would produce a reasonable profit only in industrial communities where large loan volumes were possible and comparatively large loans were in demand. They proposed a fee system. The fee system would have allowed specified charges in addition to the maximum rate and would have yielded somewhat more than 4 per cent a month. But the Russell Sage Foundation was opposed to a fee system. Its representatives argued that in the past lenders had seized on the permissibility of fees to load "oppressive" charges onto the borrower. Finally, an all-inclusive 3½ per cent a month ceiling was settled upon as a compromise.

The "per month" basis of the charge was borrowed from the earlier remedial agencies, which had found it to have several advantages. In the first place, it made special delinquency charges unnecessary since the borrower paid for each day for which he used the money. Second, it avoided the need of prepayment refunds. Third, it permitted a simple method of refinancing since loans could be enlarged, extended, or reduced, without the need of prepayment refunds. And, finally, the "per month" basis of the charge was designed to impress the borrower with the cost of the loan so that he would borrow only when necessary.

It may be argued that the borrower would have been shocked even more if the rate had been stated on an annual basis. However, the original Uniform Small Loan Act was drawn up and supported by the joint efforts of a philanthropic organization and representatives of the small loan industry. The statement of finance charges at an annual rate well above the traditional 6 per cent established in most usury laws would have about guaranteed that the proposed remedial legislation

[26] Robinson and Nugent, *op. cit.*, p. 116.

[27] Gallert, Hilborn, and May, *op. cit.*, pp. 18-88, and Robinson and Nugent, *op. cit.*, pp. 32-117.

would not have passed state legislatures. Further, it would have shocked the consumer into the arms of the loan shark, who, as we have shown, was careful to conceal his real rates.[28]

In the years immediately following 1916, modified versions of the Uniform Small Loan Law were introduced into the legislatures of a number of states. In most cases, opposition was severe. It came mostly from well-meaning citizens who were addicted to the traditional usury laws, and from illegal lenders. Yet passage of the law was effected in some states. The experience gained by the lenders governed by these laws formed the basis for the revised versions of the Uniform Law which were drafted by the Russell Sage Foundation in 1918, 1919, 1923, 1932, 1935, 1942, and finally by the National Consumer Finance Association in 1948. The original Small Loan Law and these later revisions provided the bases for the laws governing the consumer finance companies in the forty-nine states in which these lenders now operate.

The changes accomplished by the first three revisions of the Uniform Small Loan Law (hereafter referred to as USLL) were minor, but the changes made in the fifth draft (1932) were substantial. Most importantly, they established conditions precedent to the issuance of a license to conduct a small loan business under special statutory regulation.

THE FIFTH DRAFT OF THE USLL

There were three principal licensing requirements in this draft. First, the applicant was to have at least $25,000 capital available for investment in the business. Second, the supervisory official in each state was authorized to investigate "the character and fitness" of the applicant. Third, the proposed lending office had to meet a test of "convenience and advantage" to the community in which it was to be operated.

The insertion of these provisions marked a major change in philosophy. They indicated a shift away from the free market and toward greater dependence on administrative control.[29] One reason for the introduction of these licensing requirements into the model law was the belief that there were economies of scale in the small loan busi-

[28] For a more complete discussion of the reasons for the choice of the percentage per month of stating charges, see Robert W. Johnson, *Methods of Stating Consumer Finance Charges*, New York, 1961, pp. 28-29.

[29] See Rolf Nugent, "The Changing Philosophy of Small Loan Regulation," *Annals of the Academy of Political and Social Science*, March 1932, pp. 208-209.

ness.[30] The entry restrictions were designed to allow lending offices to achieve the scale of operations thought to be required for low cost lending. The second reason is best understood in light of the characteristics of the consumer loan market at that time.

For many years after 1916, the small loan market was predominantly a "seller's market." Before 1929, however, the situation began to change. This was due in part to the opening of the normal investment markets to the securities of small loan companies but it was also later aggravated by the decline in demand resulting from the Great Depression.

Late in 1928, one major company whose business was mostly in larger cities reduced its rate. Shortly afterward, a number of its competitors followed. This provided a test of the efficacy of price competition within the existing regulatory framework. Its consequences proved to be not entirely salutary. For one thing, competition was severe only for preferred classes of loans, and borrowers who needed very small sums were neglected. Competitive advertising, some overlending, and collection pressure also developed. The triple requirements of "character and fitness," "convenience and advantage," and minimum capital were based on this experience. They were designed to limit the number of loan offices and so decrease the likelihood of a recurrence of destructive price competition.[31]

The rate cuts of the late 1920's and early 1930's were taken in many states as evidence that the small loan business could be conducted at lower rates than the prevailing maxima. But this belief failed to recognize that in many cases the lower rates had led to an increase in loan sharking. Thus rate ceiling reductions followed in a number of states.

In the early 1930's, Rolf Nugent conducted a detailed study of the effects of these rate ceiling reductions in three states. He showed that they had resulted in an emphasis on larger loans with a reduction in the volume of smaller loans. Further, they caused a severe contraction in the service of licensed lenders which drove borrowers to loan sharks and to lenders in neighboring states with higher rates.[32]

[30] See Mors, *op. cit.*, Part I, p. 58.

[31] See Miller Upton, "An Economic Appraisal of Convenience and Advantage Licensing by Small-Loan Statutes, *Journal of Business*, Vol. XXV, October 1952, p. 250.

[32] Rolf Nugent, "Three Experiments with Small-Loan Interest Rates," *Harvard Business Review*, October 1933, p. 35.

For present purposes, the important innovation of the Sixth Draft of the Uniform Small Loan Law was its recommendation of a graduated maximum rate permitting a higher rate on smaller loans. The purpose of the graduated rate was twofold. First, it had been observed that when the rate limit was a single uniform maximum, lenders preferred larger loans. (The reason was that the cost of making a consumer loan, as a percentage of the principal, varies inversely with the size of the loan.) This had encouraged illegal lenders to creep back into the business of making the smaller loans. The graduated rate was designed to equalize the profitability of large and small loans.[33] Second, it created "a precise point of cleavage for further competitive rate reductions."[34] There were three alternative graduated rate devices considered.[35] One was a single or step rate; the other two were multiple rates.

Under the so-called "step" rate, a single rate is charged on the entire loan but the rate charged depends upon the size of the loan; for example, 3½ per cent a month on loans of $100 to $300 and 2 per cent per month on larger loans. The principal defects of the step rate were thought to be: first, it results in absurd differences in charges near the dividing points, e.g., in this case the borrower may pay less in dollars for a $210 loan than for a $190 loan. Also, it was claimed that it increases the temptation for licensees to lend in the most profitable denominations regardless of the applicant's needs, which is exactly the problem that was to be solved.[36]

A second device was that known as the "combination" rate. It combines an initial or periodic fee fixed in dollars with a maximum rate (in per cent) on outstanding balances. One disadvantage of this method was that it encourages the making of very small loans at onerous rates. A second disadvantage was held to be the difficulty of obtaining adequate cost data on which to base the graduated rate. But there is no reason why this holds any more strongly for the combination rate than the aggregate rate discussed below. A genuinely important dis-

[33] Robinson and Nugent, *op. cit.*, p. 266.
[34] Nugent, "The Changing Philosophy of Small Loan Legislation," p. 209.
[35] Robinson and Nugent, *op. cit.*, pp. 266-271.
[36] *Ibid.*, p. 268.

advantage, however, is that borrower comparisons of rates of different lenders is practically impossible when lenders use combination rates if both their dollar charges and percentage rates differ.

The third device is that known as the "aggregate" rate. It combines two or more rates in the regulation of charges, e.g., 3½ per cent a month on the first $100 of a loan (the lowest loan size bracket), 2½ per cent a month on the portion of the loan in excess of $100 but not exceeding $200 (the higher loan size bracket). It thus allows a given rate to be charged upon the portion of a loan less than a certain amount and a lower rate on the portion in excess of this amount. The combined rate on loans exceeding the sum at which the higher rate becomes effective is thus decreased as the loan increases in size. (This is exactly the same effect achieved under the combination rate.) This was the device agreed upon and it is the method still in effect in most states.

The 1942 and 1948 amendments to the Uniform Small Loan Law were minor. However, two main trends in regulation have developed in the post-World War II period in the states that have adopted some version of the Uniform Small Loan Law: first, there have been periodic increases in the maximum loan; second, an increasing number of states have adopted precomputation of charges and annual add-on rates (frequently graduated) and abandoned per cent per month rates. The trend toward precomputation and annual add-on rates has been aimed at improving gross revenue, operating efficiency, and borrower relations. On prepaid loans, precomputation and annual add-on produce higher gross revenue than per cent per month. This is because of differences in the procedures for allocating the finance charge to each month under these alternative methods of computing charges.[37] Also, the installment payment must be separated into finance charge and return of principal when per cent per month is used. No such separation is necessary for precomputation and annual add-on and this reportedly increases operating efficiency.[38] Finally it is claimed that borrowers prefer the equal monthly payments they get with precomputation and annual add-on to the uneven payments of per cent per month on the declining balance.[39]

[37] See John C. Wetzel, "Earned Income Under Precomputation," *Personal Finance Law Quarterly Report*, Winter 1957, pp. 7-10.

[38] See J. Miller Redfield, "Why Precomputation?" *Personal Finance Law Quarterly Report*, Spring 1960, pp. 57-59.

[39] *Loc. cit.*

CHAPTER 3

The Criteria For Evaluating Regulation

Rate ceilings and loan limits are currently in force in the consumer finance industry in New York as well as the consumer finance industries in forty-eight other states.[1] Further, judging from the final draft of the UCCC proposed by the National Conference of Commissioners on Uniform State Laws, rate regulation, if not loan size regulation, is likely to be maintained in the future.[2] The question therefore arises of just what are and should be the criteria for setting and evaluating regulatory limits. This chapter develops these criteria by reviewing and evaluating the three rate structure analyses made by the New York State Banking Department. First, however, it will be helpful to review rate setting in New York prior to the Department's rate studies.

Early Rate Setting in New York

In the late 1800's and early 1900's, New York was a leader in small loan legislation. It gave impetus to the earliest recognition of the problems involved in lending small sums by establishing the Provident Loan Society in 1894. Although the legislation that established the Provident Loan Society was limited to chartering a single institution, it initiated the trial and error experimentation, described in Chapter 2. In 1895, another small loan bill was drafted and became law. The 1895 Law, antedating the Uniform Small Loan Law by some twenty years, contained the basic elements of the latter model bill. Its chief provisions were: (1) permission to do business granted by the Banking Depart-

[1] Arkansas has no small loan law.

[2] See revised final draft of the UCCC, Commerce Clearing House Installment Credit Guide No. 191, extra ed., December 12, 1968.

ment upon the fulfillment of certain prerequisites, (2) a maximum charge, (3) limitation on the amount loaned, (4) supervision by the superintendent of banks, and (5) penalties for violation.

Although many of these provisions were later adopted in the Uniform Small Loan Law, the New York law of 1895 was a failure. The prime reason was that it was based on the mistaken belief that a large number of philanthropic organizations would be formed to meet the demand for consumer loans.[3] Thus, although the 1895 law permitted charges of 3 per cent a month for the first two months in which the loan was outstanding and a rate of 2 per cent thereafter, it provided for incorporation only of limited dividend personal loan associations.

In 1907, the Russell Sage Foundation, which played a key role in formulating later personal loan legislation, was incorporated by a special act of the New York Legislature "for the improvement of social and living conditions in the United States of America." The Foundation immediately became active in promoting small loan legislation in New York and, in 1910, a further amendment of the 1895 Law was passed.

By this time, New York had become the leading state in small loan legislation. Its position was unique in three main respects. First, New York was the only state which provided that "no other person unless coming under this statute" may charge more than provided by the general usury law. This meant that the business of lending at rates higher than permitted in the general usury laws was confined to licensees. Second, New York was the only state which provided for really effective law enforcement by penalizing violations of nonlicensees. Not only were forfeiture of interest and principal of the nonlicensee's transactions provided for, but there was also a criminal penalty for such lending. And third, New York was the only state which charged a particular state official with enforcement of the law.

In 1913, the development of small loan legislation in New York, based upon amendments of the 1895 law, took an unexpected turn. Numerous changes and amendments were made that practically nullified all previous enactments and reduced the authorized maximum rate of charge. Deficiencies of this 1913 act raised a storm of protest from the New York Bar Association, legal aid societies, New York newspapers, the Russell Sage Foundation, and many other institu-

[3] New York State Banking Department, *Special Report of the Superintendent of Banks on Licensed Lenders,* 1946, p. 8.

tions. As a result, in 1914 a revised bill, sponsored by the Russell Sage Foundation and the New York State Banking Department, was incorporated in the Banking Law as Article IX. The 1914 act provided for a rate of 2 per cent a month on unpaid principal balances and fees, which brought the total charge to approximately 2¼ percent a month on average. However, it failed to attract substantial additional capital. In 1914, there were only 20 lenders operating under Article IX and by 1929 the number of licensed lenders had fallen to 17.

Although many states adopted the provisions of the Uniform Small Loan Law very shortly after it had been drafted in 1916, it was not until 1932 that New York finally passed a modified version of this law.

In 1928, New York had been shocked by disclosures of loan shark operations on a large scale. It was estimated that $25 million of usurious charges at rates ranging from 240 to 520 per cent had been taken that year from New York City wage earners alone, and the press ran scare headlines about the problem.[4]

The legislature, in response to the State Attorney General's plea for action, delegated authority to the Baumes Crime Commission to conduct an investigation of the problem. When the Commission made its report, it pointed out that:

> As presently constituted the New York Personal Loan Law has two chief defects which the changes recommended seek to remedy. They are:
>
> (a) Insufficient rate.[5]
>
> (b) Burdensome restrictions on licensees and the granting of licenses.
>
> Capital, if allowed a fair return, should flow into the business contemplated by the Personal Loan Law as freely as it has into other varieties of lending.[6]

After investigating the problem, the Attorney General's special committee reported that it found a very pressing need for legitimate sources of small loans. The committee proposed to meet this need by making the New York law similar to the Uniform Small Loan Law.

In 1929, 1930, and 1931, bills were introduced in the legislature to revise the New York Small Loan Law along the lines recommended by the committee. But, despite support from the Baumes Crime

[4] New York State Consumer Finance Association, *The Consumer Finance Business*, 1954, p. 13.

[5] The rate under the existing statute was 2 per cent per month plus a fee. See New York Association of Personal Finance Companies, *Small Loan Legislation in New York*, 1938, p. 17.

[6] *Loc. cit.*

TABLE 1

Rate Ceilings and Loan Limits of the New York Small Loan Law, 1932-1969

Year	Rate Structure
1932[a]	3-2½ per cent at $150 to $300
1941	2½-2 per cent at $100 to $300
1949	2½-2 per cent at $100; ½ per cent at $300 to $500
1960	2½-2 per cent at $100; ¾ per cent at $300 to $800
1969	2½-2 per cent at $100; 1½ per cent at $300 to $900; 1¼ per cent at $900 to $1,400.

NOTE: All rates quoted here are monthly rates and apply to that part of the loan balance as indicated. Thus the 1932 rate was 3 per cent per month on that part of the loan balance up to $150, and 2 per cent per month on that part of the loan balance from $150 up to $300.

[a] Immediately prior to the passage of the New York Small Loan Law the maximum rate of charge was 2 per cent per month, plus fees.

Commission, the State Banking Department, the Russell Sage Foundation, the Attorney General's committee, and other agencies, the bills failed to pass. However, in 1932, a modified version of the Uniform Small Loan Law was again introduced into the New York legislature and was finally passed.

The New York Small Loan Statute as passed in 1932 was intended to be a "borrower's law." It increased the permissible rate of charge to 3 per cent per month on the first $150 of the unpaid balance of the loan and 2½ per cent per month on any amount in excess of $150 up to $300. The $300 loan limit had been in force since 1920 and was retained in the 1932 law.

Since 1932, the rate ceilings and loan limits of the New York Small Loan Law have been revised four times, as summarized in Table 1. The criteria on which the first three of these rate revisions were based will be reviewed and evaluated below. The fourth revision occurred after this study had been completed.

The First Rate Study

The State Banking Department's first rate study was conducted in 1940.[7] It was directed primarily at determining whether the maximum rates prescribed in the New York Small Loan Statute of 1932 were justified in light of the industry's income and expense experience.

[7] New York State Banking Department, *Special Report Relative to Licensed Lenders*, 1940.

The 1940 rate study may be classified into two parts. The first analyzed earnings and expenses by (1) type of licensee (national chains, state chains, and independents); (2) size of community; (3) average size of loans; and (4) average size of offices. The Department concluded that (1) type of licensee has relatively little effect upon profitability; (2) offices in small communities are more profitable than offices in large cities; (3) net earning rates tend generally to increase with the size of loans; and (4) large offices cost less and are more profitable than small offices.

The second part of the study was directed specifically at evaluating the adequacy of rate ceilings. No attention was given to the loan limit. The recommendation of a rate ceiling decrease and specific rate ceiling changes were a result of the Department study.

First, the Department compared rates actually charged with the rate ceilings and found that more than 60 per cent of the total volume of loans in 1938 was made at rates lower than the ceiling rates.

Second, the Department argued that a rate of return of about 7 per cent on assets employed in the small loan business was fair and reasonable and adequate to encourage the continued employment of capital already invested in the small loan field. On the basis of judgment, the total costs of making loans in 1938 were separated into costs incident to the dollar amount of loans made and costs incident to the number of loans made. Dividing these costs by the dollar value and number of loans made, respectively, the cost per dollar loaned was computed as 1.0259 per cent per month and the cost per loan made was found to be $0.6465. An extra charge was added to this cost to develop the rate of charge necessary to yield lenders a return of 7 per cent on total assets employed.

The Department then calculated that a charge of 2½ per cent per month on loan balances not exceeding $100 and 2 per cent per month on balances in excess of $100 would enable lenders to achieve the required 7 per cent return on total assets employed.

Based upon its analysis of costs and earnings by type of lender and location, the Department considered the probable effect of the recommended rate change upon (1) the profitability of different types of lenders, and (2) the geographical distribution of branch offices. The conclusions arrived at were:

> (1) Earnings rates in excess of 11 percent would be eliminated with the exception of four licensees. On the other hand, the proportion of loan volume yielding less than 4 percent on employed assets, would be in-

creased from 2 percent to 12 percent. The most marked change in this respect would be in the local and minor national chain groups.[8]

(2) The virtual elimination of the highest earning group in all places other than those of less than 30,000 population . . . [such that] in each locational group, the majority of licensees and the bulk of loan volume would fall into the earning range of from 4 percent to 9.99 percent.[9]

(3) The median rate of net earnings [for offices] is reduced from 11.3 percent to 7.3 percent.[10]

Evaluation

The historical development of small loan legislation was surveyed in Chapter 2 and the earlier part of this chapter. It showed that the principal function of this legislation is to attract legitimate capital into the small loan field in sufficient quantities to eliminate loan sharking. History also shows that to perform this function it is necessary that small loan legislation permit licensed lenders the opportunity to earn reasonable profits. "Reasonable" profits are those that are commensurate with operating costs and the risk of the business and in line with profit potentials available in other comparable enterprises.

The Characteristics of Loans and Borrowers. Since the ultimate objective of the small loan statute is to eliminate loan sharking, the principal test of the efficacy of regulation should be a measure of the extent of loan sharking. However, it is particularly difficult to obtain this measure. Accordingly, the Department cannot be criticized severely for failing to estimate the prevalence of loan sharking. The Department may be criticized, however, for its failure to analyze the characteristics of loans made by the licensed lenders to ascertain whether these lenders were meeting the kind of demand contemplated by the statute.

Similarly, an analysis of borrower characteristics may have been fruitful. It may have shown, e.g., that, over a period of time, the pressure of inflation on costs and the downward trend of average rates (which results as average loan size increases within a graduated rate structure) forced lenders to curtail loan services to the less risky borrowers (those who were rejected possibly turned to loan sharks as a result). The Department recognized that the small loan law was aimed to serve a particular class of borrowers. In its words, the law

[8] *Ibid.*, p. 20.
[9] *Loc. cit.*
[10] *Loc. cit.*

was designed to serve "borrowers who are unable to meet the credit or security requirements of other institutions." Yet it conducted no analysis of the effect of the prevailing and recommended rate structure upon the class of borrowers who obtain credit.

The only characteristic of the credit services examined in the first rate study was the rates which lenders were actually charging. These were compared with the rate ceilings under the theory that, if the rate ceilings were too high, actual rates would be lower than the maximum allowed rates. By arguing that competition would hold rates below the ceiling if the ceiling were higher than necessary to attract capital, the Department was implicitly accepting that competition could be an effective regulator of rates. And, if competition can effectively regulate rates, the question arises of why establish rate ceilings at all. Further, if a rate ceiling is to be judged too high when lenders charge less than the ceiling rate, then lenders will clearly have an incentive not to charge less than the permitted maximum. When coupled with the test that lenders are to earn only reasonable net returns, this test of the adequacy of the rate structure can serve not only to promote high rates but also to discourage lenders from striving to achieve operating economies.

The Adequacy of Lending Facilities. As noted earlier, the goal of legislation is not merely to see that a particular class of loans is made. The goal of legislation is also to ensure that sufficient quantities of this kind of credit are extended legally to meet the demand of borrowers. It is appropriate, therefore, to evaluate the volume of lending facilities. However, in the 1940 study, the Department gave only cursory attention to the problem of measuring the adequacy of lending facilities. The Department was content to note only that the number of loan branches and amount of loans outstanding had grown and that there were lenders in most communities. No attention was given to changes in the number of lenders, as opposed to loan branches,[11] or changes in the number or amount of loans made.

However, the Department's failure to measure the number of lenders in the state is not serious. First, the main objective of small loan legislation is to drive out loan sharking. For this purpose, it is necessary only that loan facilities be available from legal lenders throughout the state. Hence, the number of loan branches is a better

[11] As used here, a "lender" is a lending firm that may have one or more outlets or "loan branches."

measure of the availability of lending facilities than the number of lenders. Second, the number of lenders might have been measured to ascertain whether there was greater concentration in the industry than might be deemed desirable. The Department effectively met this second purpose by analyzing the breakdown of lenders into locals, state chains, and national chains.

The failure of the Department to analyze the effect of the rate structure upon the number and amount of loans made is more serious. These are perhaps the most relevant measures of the quantity of lending facilities made available under the enabling statutes. The amount of loans outstanding might have grown as a result of a lengthening of the average maturity of loans, even if the volume of loan facilities supplied had decreased. Hence, the amount of loans outstanding, the measure used by the Department, is a highly imperfect measure of the volume of loan facilities supplied.

Earnings. The main concern of the study was whether lenders were earning adequate or excessive profits. Analysis of earnings rates can be important because low earnings may foretell a shrinkage in the supply of loan facilities. Also, since a prime objective of regulation is to replace the high rate loan shark by lower rate legal lenders, licensed lenders should not be permitted to charge rates higher than those required to ensure the supply of adequate facilities into the business.

However, if competition is effective, it will force adjustment of the characteristics and volume of the credit service supplied to the point where lenders cannot earn excessive profits. The level of earnings will then not vary with the rate structure and earnings will not be a useful basis for evaluating the rate structure. In fact, under these conditions, changing the rate structure will have no impact on earnings, after an adjustment period, and will affect only the characteristics and volume of the credit service. However, in the absence of competitive pressures strong enough to force adjustment of the credit characteristics and volume of credit to the rate structure, earnings may vary with the rate structure. Rate structure changes may, under these conditions, reduce rates and earnings without otherwise affecting the industry.

Thus, whether earnings rates are a useful criterion for judging the rate structure depends on how perfectly competition forces the industry to adjust to its rate structure. There are two possible ways of ascertaining the extent of these adjustments. The first, that employed by the Department, requires knowledge of what normal earnings are for the industry. The Department assumed this to be 7 per cent on assets. It is not clear how this standard was developed, although it could reasonably have been derived from comparisons with other regulated or unregulated industries. If it is found that lenders earn more than this standard, then it may be assumed that adjustments to the rate structure are imperfect and rates can be reduced without affecting the characteristics and volume of the credit service. The second test of the extent of industry adjustments is more direct. It involves analysis of whether the industry has actually adjusted its loan characteristics and volume of lending facilities to the rate structure, and whether earnings rates in fact vary with rate structure changes.

To sum up, the earnings criterion is useful only if the industry has not adjusted to its rate structure and earns more than normal profits. The extent of the industry's adjustments may be judged either by evaluating the industry's earnings or by direct study of its adjustment to its rate structure. The Department failed to do either. First, it did not specify how its 7 per cent standard was developed. Second, the Department, as noted, made little direct analysis of whether the industry had adjusted to its rate structure and hence whether rate reductions would bring about reductions in earnings rates as projected, or would merely result in further industry adjustments.

It is true that the probable impact of the rate structure change on lender and branch office populations was considered. But the effects of the rate structure change on the characteristics of the credit service and borrowers who would obtain credit were not considered in any detail. Nor was the probable impact of the rate structure change on the number and dollar volume of loans examined. Nevertheless, we may turn now to the specific recommendations made by the Department on the basis of its earnings analysis. The relationships between industry adjustments and earnings rates will be taken up again in Chapters 5-7.

On the basis of its earnings analysis, the Department recommended rates of 2½-2 per cent at $100 and $300, recognizing that the projected yield under this rate structure "falls short of the calculated cost plus profit rates on loan balances of less than about $90 and exceeds by a small margin the calculated cost plus profit rates on larger loan balances."[12] The Department reasoned that "this margin should enable

[12] New York State Banking Department, *Special Report Relative to Licensed Lenders*, 1940, p. 19.

the lender to compensate for the inadequacy of the rate permitted to be charged on very small loans."[13]

This reasoning is specious. If lenders can just earn fair profits by making loans of all sizes permitted, and if some of these loans are unprofitable to make, then it should be expected that the unprofitable loans would not be made. This would permit the lenders to earn higher profits, at least until a rate reduction is enforced.[14]

The Second Rate Study

The Banking Department's second rate study was conducted in 1946.[15] The consumer finance industry had just gone through a period of sharply decreasing loan volume. It was then entering a phase in which a reversal of this trend appeared likely to develop as the supply of consumer goods began its postwar increase. It was, therefore, a pivotal time for lenders. Further, developments during the war, for example, changes in price levels and in wages and salaries, made it desirable, in the opinion of the Department, to reevaluate existing maximum limits on loan sizes at that time.

The legal maximum loan size was evaluated on the following basis:

> In New York State the policy has been to confine licensed lender activity to the small loan borrower. The Department knows of no reason why this policy should be modified. The effort has been to determine whether, in view of price and income payment changes over the last several years, licensed lenders are now able to meet the loan requirements of the person of modest income, particularly the wage earner.[16]

Analysis of changes in potential borrowers' incomes and in the consumer price level led the Department to recommend an increase in the loan limit to $500.

[13] *Ibid.*

[14] It is possible that the Department meant that very small loans would be unprofitable at the permitted rate if lenders made only very small loans, but that these small loans could be made profitably on a marginal basis, i.e., that these small loans would add to profits if lenders also made larger loans. However, this does not appear to have been the sense of the Department's report, which is admittedly somewhat ambiguous on this point.

[15] New York State Banking Department, *Special Report Relative to Licensed Lenders, New York*, 1946.

[16] *Ibid.*, p. 10.

As in the 1940 rate study, rates actually charged were compared with the rate ceilings. But whereas in 1940 most loans were made at less than the maximum rates, it was now found that 270 of the 279 offices were charging the maximum rate. Rates in New York were also compared to rates in other states. The Department noted with apparent satisfaction that "it can be said that borrowers from small loan companies in New York State pay less interest, with only two minor exceptions, than in any other state."[17]

However, the crucial test of the adequacy of the rate ceilings was again, as in 1940, the net earnings rates of lenders. Net earnings were measured as a percentage of loans outstanding, total assets, used and useful assets, and total capital and equity capital. Their trends were analyzed and net earnings on total capital for licensed lenders were compared with net earnings on total capital for leading corporations. From this comparison, the Department concluded that licensed lender earnings were "not excessive."

However, the Department predicted that with the "recommended increase in the loan limit from $300 to $500, the earnings of licensed lenders will be affected to such an extent that a reduction in rates becomes possible and advisable."[18]

This reasoning was elaborated as follows:

> The Department has indicated that it does not believe the licensed lenders need a higher net profit than they are now receiving to make the small loan field in New York State an attractive outlet for capital. With the larger interest income that would come to the lenders from the proposed increase in the loan limit, and with no additional costs, the way would be opened to recommend a cut in the loan rates.[19]

The Department then estimated specifically that, with the expected loan size distribution under a maximum loan limit of $500, a gross charge of approximately 23.5 per cent a year would provide lenders with an average net return, after taxes, of about 6 per cent on total capital. This was the rate that the Department considered would ensure the maintenance of an adequate amount of facilities to handle the small loan demand in the state.

[17] *Ibid.*, p. 7.
[18] *Ibid.*, p. 21.
[19] *Loc. cit.*

The Department held further that:

> The best adjustment of rates [to yield the required 6 percent after taxes on total capital] from the standpoint of public policy would be to reduce the present charge of 2½ percent on amounts up to $100 to 2 percent, thereby making the 2 percent rate applicable to all amounts of $300 or less. On the unpaid balances above $300 permitted by the increase of the loan-size limit to $500, the rate should be 1 percent.[20]

Evaluation

As in the comments on the 1940 rate study, this evaluation will focus upon the Department's analysis of borrowers and loan characteristics, the adequacy of lending facilities, and earnings rates. As noted earlier, given the objectives of regulation, these are the appropriate considerations for evaluating the rate structure (including loan limits.)

Borrower and Loan Characteristics. The 1946 study failed to analyze in any depth the characteristics of borrowers served by the consumer finance industry. It noted only that "the available information [which was not supplied] shows that to a large extent borrowers from licensed lenders are recruited from the low income groups which they were intended to accommodate."[21]

However, the 1946 study did consider the average size of loans made and the adequacy of the loan limit in the light of the growing demand for larger loans. Its tests of the adequacy of the loan limit were logical and consistent with the legislative objective of meeting from legal sources a given class of demand for credit. The Department reasoned that if the loan limit were not raised, the industry would not be able to continue to service the demand for loans of given purposes (as inflation was pushing the amounts of many of these loans above the legal limit). Also, the Department recognized that, as the borrowers served by the consumer finance industry continued to experience increases in income, they would demand larger loans for the higher priced items that they could afford. The inability of the industry to meet the demand for these loans and from these borrowers could only benefit the loan sharks, who were the sole alternative source of supply for this kind of credit.

[20] *Loc. cit.*
[21] *Ibid.*, p. 9.

The Adequacy of Lending Facilities. In measuring the adequacy of lending facilities, the 1946 study is only a minor improvement over the 1940 rate study. In an Appendix, it provides abundant statistical data on trends in the numbers of lenders and loan branches and the numbers and amount of loans made. However, these are not analyzed in the text. They are referred to only once as "the data covering the expansion of licensed lender volume since 1932" and showing that "the number of licensed lender offices reached a peak . . . in 1941 . . . and thereafter declined to 270 at the end of 1944."[22] Actually, however, the data in the Appendix show a fairly systematic decline after 1941 not merely in the number of lenders, but also the number of loan offices and the number and amount of loans made.

Earnings. As in its 1940 study, the Department failed, in its 1946 study, to get to the crux of the issue of what earnings indicate about the adequacy of the rate structure. The Department found earnings to be reasonable, which may be *prima facie* evidence of competitive adjustments to the rate structure and the irrelevance of earnings as a criterion for evaluating rates. However, since the Department made no detailed analysis of the effects of the rate structure on the industry's performance other than its earnings performance, it is impossible to tell exactly what significance should have been attached to the earnings criterion. As in its 1940 study, the Department appeared bent primarily on preventing lenders from earning what might be considered excessive profits. It did not give due attention to the problem that rate structure changes designed to stave off excess profitability might choke off the supply of credit facilities.

In any case, the legislation finally enacted did not agree with the Department's judgment on what were adequate earnings rates or what would be the best rate structure to yield these earnings. The Department recommended a reduction from 2½ to 2 per cent per month in the permissible rates on loans up to $300, and a rate of 1 per cent per month on loans above $300. But the law finally enacted consisted of a rate of 2½ per cent per month on loans up to $100, 2 per cent per month for the part of the loan balance between $100 and $300, and ½ per cent per month on the portion of the loan balance in excess of $300.

[22] *Loc. cit.*

The Third Rate Study

The immediate stimulus to the detailed analysis of the licensed lender industry by the Department in 1958 [23] was the introduction into the state legislature, on February 19, 1957, of a bill sponsored by the New York State Consumer Finance Association. The bill sought an increase in the rate ceilings above $300 to 1 per cent a month from the existing ½ per cent per month, and an increase in the loan limit from $500 to $1,000. The industry's proposal was to leave unchanged the rate charges on balances up to $300.

The Department began its 1958 rate structure analysis with a review of trends in the numbers of lenders and lending offices, and loan volumes as measured by the numbers and dollar amounts of loans made. (Also, interspersed throughout its analysis are comparisons of loans outstanding in New York with loans outstanding in other states and loans outstanding held by commercial banks, credit unions, and industrial banks in New York State.) Having reviewed the changing volume of lending facilities in the state, the Banking Department then turned to a specific analysis of the adequacy of rate ceilings and loan limits.

In its analysis of the adequacy of the existing loan limit, the Department spelled out its guiding principle as follows: "Loan ceilings . . . can have little significance in an absolute sense unless to provide borrowers command over a given amount of purchasing power, and second, to limit debt commitments to their ability to repay."[24] Again, therefore, as in the 1946 study, evidence was presented on the decline in the purchasing power of the loan limit established in 1949 and changes in prospective borrowers' ability to bear indebtedness. In addition, the Department considered the effect of a restrictive loan limit on "doubling up" – the practice among borrowers of making loans at more than one lender when the amount that they want to borrow is larger than the loan limit. The Department also analyzed the probable impact of a loan limit increase on the size distribution of loans that would be made.

However, after pointing to these factors and implying that a loan limit increase would be desirable, the Department concluded as follows:

[23] New York State Banking Department, *An Analysis of the Licensed Lender Industry*, New York, 1958.

[24] *Ibid.*, pp. 12-13.

> Whatever the realities which may imply a [loan] ceiling increase, it is believed that a number of states in setting very high ceilings apparently have either unknowingly violated or ignored the precepts inherent in the meaning *small loan* industry. Not to be overlooked in any deliberations are the original purposes of small loan legislation which would militate against overly liberalized ceilings.[25]

The Department's evaluation of rate ceilings focused on the causes for the downward trends of the ratios of net income before interest to average loans outstanding, average balance sheet assets, and total capital (giving consideration to differential results by class of licensee). The Department then noted that while net earnings had declined quite persistently by each of these measures, net returns on equity had declined between 1950 and 1953, but remained constant from 1953-57. The Department compared the lower earnings levels at which the industry had stabilized with the earnings of national samples of companies in other industries. It concluded "there appears to be little ground for belief that investors in the small loan industry are at a disadvantage relative to those venturing risk capital in other industries."[26] However, the Department appeared uncertain as to what regulatory policy should follow from these divergent earnings trends and was prepared to state only that "it is apparent . . . that the earnings picture does not point decisively in any one direction."[27]

Evaluation

The 1958 rate structure study is a major improvement over the preceding studies in three main respects. First, it gave more detailed attention to the characteristics of loans made. However, like the preceding studies, it failed to analyze the impact of the rate structure upon the characteristics of borrowers who were obtaining credit. Second, unlike the previous studies, the 1958 study reviewed in detail the trends in the volume of lending facilities, as measured by the number of lenders and loan branches and the numbers and amounts of loans made. However, even the 1958 study made no attempt to uncover exactly what effect different rate ceilings and loan limits would have on the volume of lending facilities as measured in these ways.

[25] *Ibid.*, p. 3.
[26] *Ibid.*, p. 43.
[27] *Ibid.*, p. 69.

Third, the 1958 analysis of earnings was far more thorough than the earnings analyses of the previous studies. It recognized that earnings may decline as a percentage of assets without declining as a percentage of equity. It also noted that increased "trading on the equity" was the main reason net earnings on equity were held constant while net earnings on various asset bases had declined.

However, the 1958 analysis failed to face up to the question of just how far "trading on equity" could be continued. Further, it ignored the important fact that a constant level of net income on equity declines in attractiveness to investors as their risk increases from increased "trading on the equity." Even more important, the Department still held that earnings should be the principal criterion in evaluating the rate structure, even though there was considerable doubt as to whether earnings were excessive. The possibility that the industry had adjusted to its rate structure and would respond to rate structure changes only by adjusting further – with the rate structure change having, as a result, no effect on its earnings – was not faced.[28]

Chapters 5-7 seek to remedy this deficiency. They deal with the extent of the industry's adjustments to its rate structure in New York. First, however, the New York regulation is put in perspective by reviewing, in Chapter 4, the national pattern of regulation.

[28] The main exception to this generalization is that the impact of a rising average loan size on average revenues and average costs (hence on net earnings) was considered.

CHAPTER 4

The National Pattern of Regulation

In the following three chapters, the effects of rate ceilings and loan limits on the character and volume of loans and lending facilities and the earnings of lenders in the New York consumer finance industry will be analyzed. The analysis will be based in part upon comparisons among states. Therefore, it will be helpful to compare the rate ceilings and loan limits imposed on consumer finance companies in the various states. First, however, the levels of consumer finance companies' rate ceilings and loan limits will be put in perspective by comparing them with the rate ceilings and loan limits of competing lenders.

The Relative Levels of Rate Ceilings and Loan Limits

A summary of the 1964 rate ceilings and loan limits governing credit unions and commercial banks in New York and consumer finance companies in all states is provided in Appendixes A and B. It is shown that, in New York State, consumer finance companies' rate ceilings are higher but their loan limits are lower than those of credit unions and commercial banks. This pattern of regulation is found in most states.

In 1964, forty-five states set limits on the sizes of loans that the consumer finance industry could legally make.[1] These limits ranged from $300 (Alabama, Hawaii, Louisiana, Maryland, Oklahoma, Rhode Island, Tennessee, and Wisconsin) to $5,000 (California).[2] Twenty-four states had higher loan limits, seventeen states had lower loan limits, and three states (Illinois, Kentucky, and West Virginia) had the same loan limit as New York.

[1] Arkansas had no small loan law. Delaware, Mississippi, Missouri, and South Carolina placed no maximum on the industry's loan size.

[2] The vast majority of California consumer finance companies operate under the Personal Property Brokers Law, which is referred to here. Only a few companies operate under the Small Loan Law, which had a $300 ceiling in 1964.

Because the rate ceilings that apply to consumer finance companies are graduated differently in the various states, the relative levels of these ceilings can be meaningfully analyzed only by examining them over a range of loans of different sizes. This is done in Chart 1.

In constructing Chart 1, states were ranked on the basis of their rate ceilings on loans of $100, with the highest rate states being ranked first. The ceiling rates for loans of $100, $300, $500, and $800 were then plotted in Part A for states which ranked first, second, twenty-third, and twenty-fourth; Part B includes states which ranked third, fourth, twenty-fifth, and twenty-sixth; and so on.[3] On this basis, New York ranked thirty-eighth.

The procedure used to compare rates in Chart 1 permits easy visual comparison of states that have similar rate ceilings (for example, Alaska and Hawaii) and states which have widely differing rate ceilings (for example, Alaska and Kentucky) on $100 loans. In general the chart reveals that: (1) in some cases, states that have relatively high rate ceilings on small loans have relatively low rate ceilings on larger loans (for example, compare Nevada and Georgia, Part C); and (2) some states have higher rate ceilings than other states over the full range of loan sizes considered (for example, compare Alaska and Kentucky, Part A). Put differently, there is no invariable rule that states which have relatively high rate ceilings on small loans have relatively low (or offsettingly low) rate ceilings on large loans.

The relationship between the level of rate ceilings and that of loan limits was also investigated. Because each state has not one rate ceiling but a graduation of rate ceilings (which vary with the size of loan), the loan limits were compared with rate ceilings on loans of four sizes – $100, $300, $500, and $800. This range includes the loan sizes most commonly made in most states and extends up to the maximum loan size permitted in New York State. As shown in Equations 4-1 to 4-4 in Table 2, there was found to be no significant correlation at the 0.05 level[4] between the level of loan limits and the legal rate on loans of $100, $300, $500, or $800. In other words, states with high or low loan limits might have either high or low rate ceilings.

[3] The lines joining the legal rate on $100 loans to the legal rate on $300 loans, etc., in each chart reflect the continuity in the change in rate which results from the particular form of graduation of rates specified in the small loan laws.

[4] In this study, relationships are judged to be significant only at the 0.05 level.

CHART 1

The Relationship Between Legal Rate and Loan Sizes, 1964

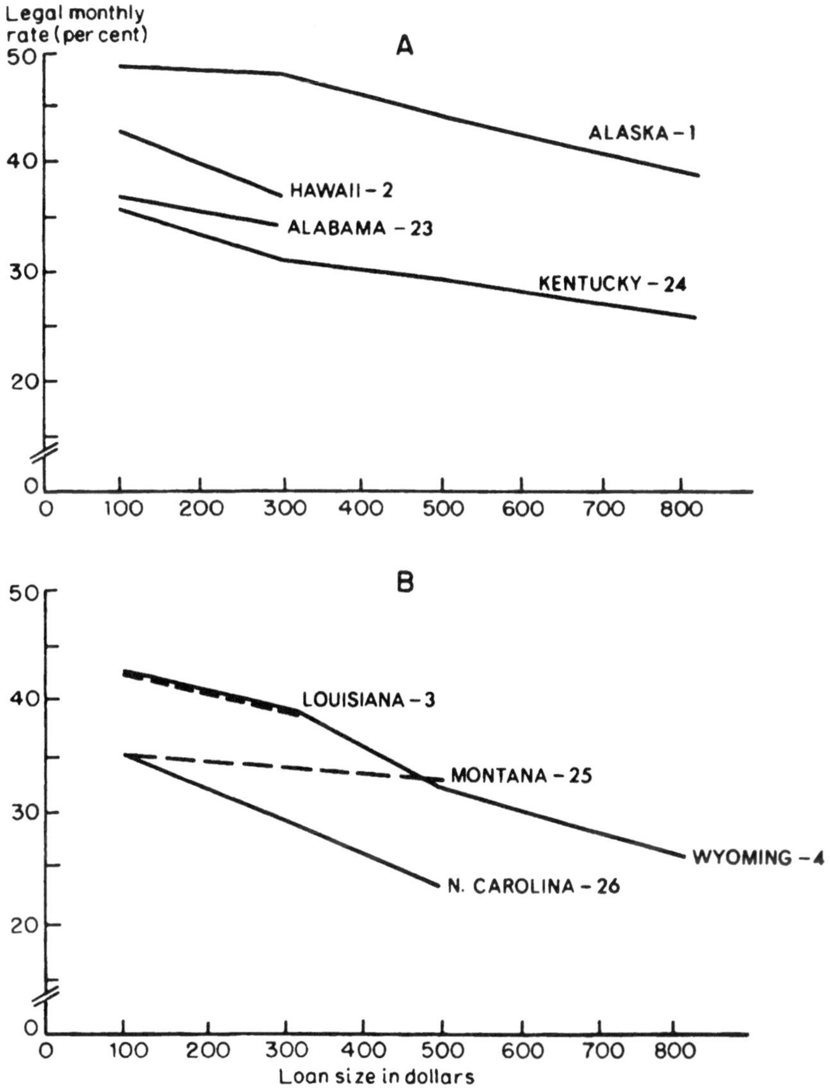

(continued)

CHART 1 (continued)

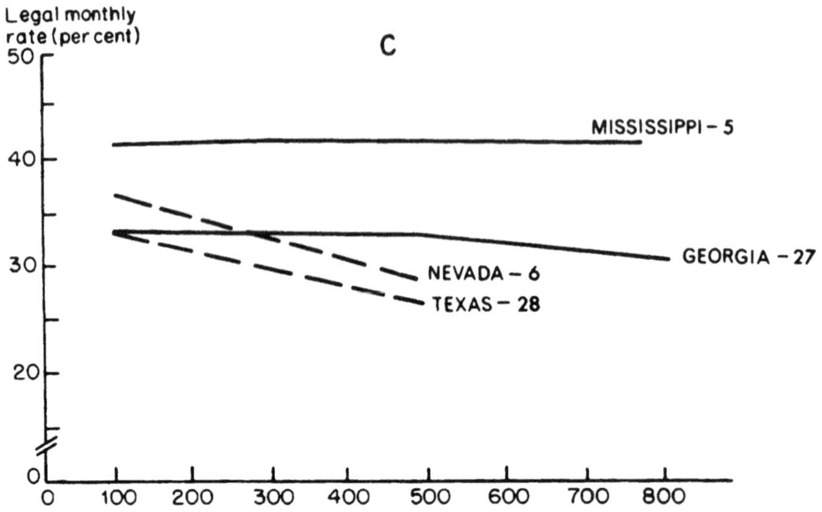

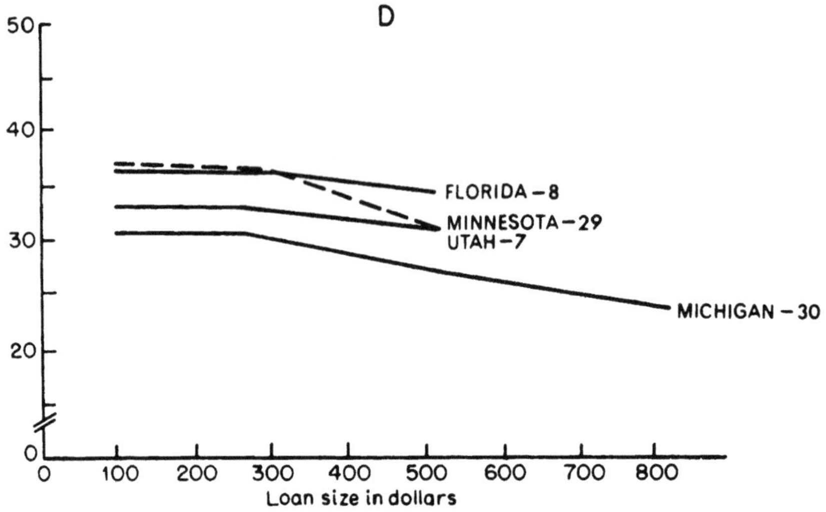

(continued)

CHART 1 (continued)

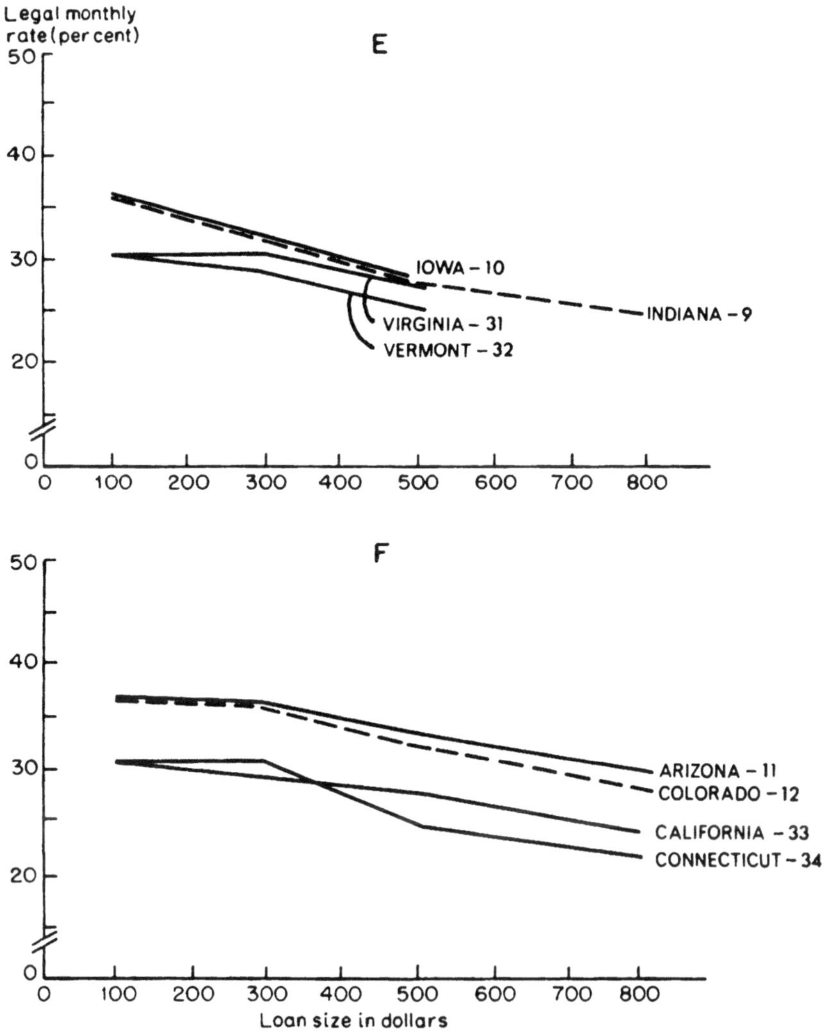

(continued)

CHART 1 (continued)

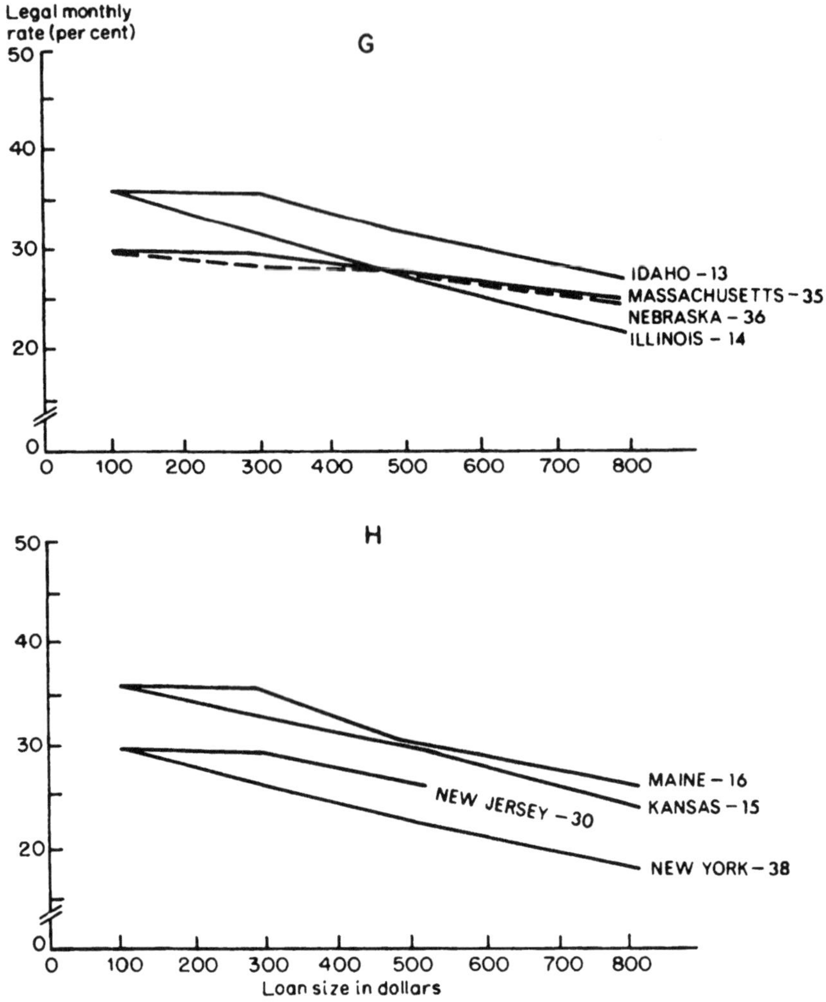

(continued)

CHART 1 (continued)

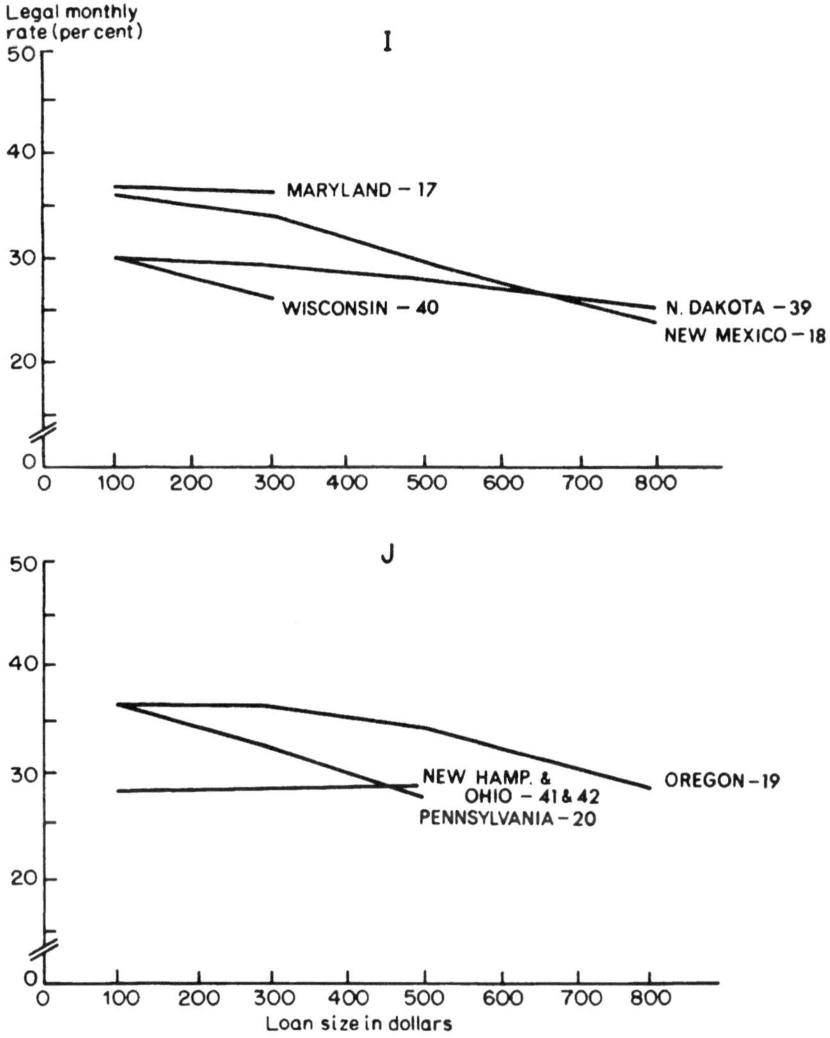

(continued)

CHART 1 (concluded)

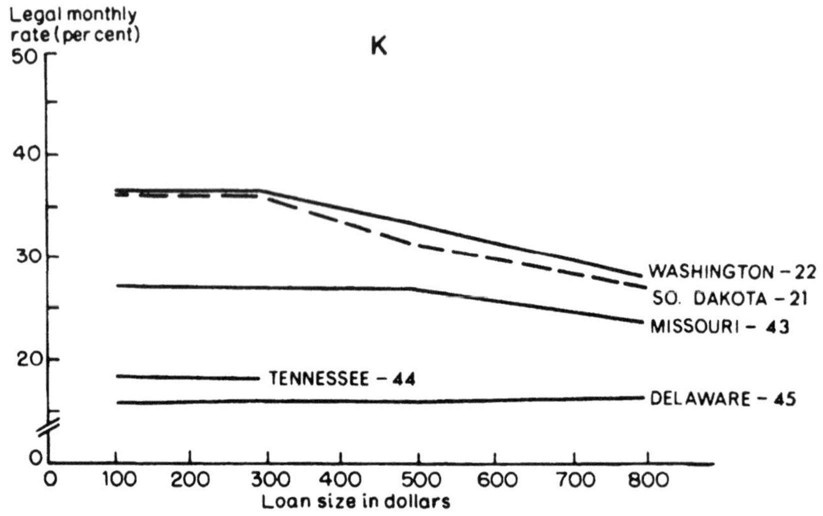

NOTE: In all cases, a twelve-month equal instalment contract is assumed. All states for which data were available are included. Rates were not computed for loans that are larger than the loan ceiling in any state. For example, in Alabama the 1964 loan ceiling was $300, and legal rates for that state are given only for loans of $300 or less.

SOURCE: From data compiled by Charles H. Gushee, Financial Publishing Company, in a mimeographed table of legal rates, supplied to the author on November 9, 1966.

TABLE 2

Rate Ceilings and Loan Limits

Equation	States[a]	Dependent Variable	Constant Term	Independent Variables, Coefficients, and Standard Errors	R^2
4-1	42	X_1	23.00	$-0.32\ X_2$ (0.30)	0.03
4-2	36	X_1	14.65	$-0.09\ X_3$ (0.36)	0.00
4-3	36	X_1	10.96	$0.08\ X_4$ (0.42)	0.00
4-4	22	X_1	19.54	$-0.12\ X_5$ (0.60)	0.00

NOTE: X_1 = the loan limit (in hundreds of dollars); X_2 = the interest ceiling on $100 loans (in per cent per annum); X_3 = the interest ceiling on $300 loans (in per cent per annum); X_4 = the interest ceiling on $500 loans (in per cent per annum); and X_5 = the interest ceiling on $800 loans (in per cent per annum).

[a] The state is the unit of observation.

The two main observations in this section are worth repeating as they hold the key to understanding some of the findings in Chapter 5. They are (1) some states have higher rate ceilings than other states throughout the range of permitted loan sizes; and (2) there is no correlation between the general level of a state's rate ceilings and the level of its loan limit.

The first generalization makes it possible to classify states such as Alaska as high rate ceiling states and states such as New York as relatively low rate ceiling states and to study the effects of the different rate ceilings in these states. This is substantially more difficult in those cases where a state has relatively high rate ceilings on small loans but relatively low rate ceilings on larger loans.

The second generalization makes it easier to separate the effects of rate ceilings from those of loan limits. This would not have been possible if high rates were systematically associated with, say, low loan limits. It should be pointed out, however, that this lack of systematic relationship between the rate ceiling and the loan limit does not completely eliminate the problem of studying the separate effects of rate ceilings and loan limits. While rate ceilings and loan limits are not correlated, average rates charged and average sizes of loans made are inversely correlated (as will be shown in Chapter 5).

The Frequency of Rate Structure Revisions

In the period 1955-64, New York had one rate structure change, in 1960. It involved (a) an increase in the permissible rate on loans larger than $300, and (b) an increase in the loan limit from $500 to $800. By way of comparison, the rate structures of the forty-two states for which data were available were studied over the 1955-64 period to ascertain the nature and frequency of the revisions made in this ten year period. It was found that:

There were twenty states with no rate structure change.[5]

There were twenty-two states with rate structure changes. Sixteen states had one rate structure change, of which two had only a loan limit change, two had only a rate ceiling change,[6] and twelve had both a loan limit and a rate ceiling change. Six states had two rate structure changes. In the first rate structure change, one state had only a loan limit change; one state had only a rate ceiling change; and four states had both a loan limit change and a rate ceiling change. In the second rate structure change, three states had only a loan limit change; one state had only a rate ceiling change; and two had both a loan limit change and a rate ceiling change.

Of the twenty-four loan limit changes, all twenty-four were increases. Of the twenty-two rate ceiling changes, two were increases (South Dakota, 1956, and Indiana, 1960); two were decreases (New Mexico, 1961, and Nebraska, 1963); and eighteen were new rates on new or enlarged highest loan brackets.

Entry Regulations

The principal barriers to entry into the consumer finance industry are the earlier mentioned convenience and advantage (hereafter called

[5] A rate structure change refers to any change (increase or decrease) in either the legal rate limit, or the loan ceiling, or both.

[6] A rate ceiling change is defined as either a change in the legal rate without a change in the loan limit, or a new rate on the new or enlarged highest loan bracket. An example of a new rate on the enlarged highest loan bracket is the 1960 rate structure change in New York State. The rate structure in this case was changed from 2½ per cent at $100, ½ per cent at $300 to $500; to 2½-2 per cent at $100, ¾ per cent at $300 to $800. The new rate is ¾ per cent, changed from ½ per cent. The enlarged highest loan bracket is $300 to $800, changed from $500 to $800.

CA) provisions in the statutes that govern consumer finance companies in some states. Of the forty-nine states in which consumer finance companies operated in 1964, thirty-three, including New York, had CA provisions. However, regulatory agencies are reported to vary widely from state to state in the stringency with which they apply these provisions. In some CA states, entry is reported to be practically impossible; whereas, in other CA states entry is as unrestricted as in non-CA states. There is no really satisfactory measure of the stringency of application; nor does there appear to be any measure that represents a significant improvement over the broad classification of states on the basis of whether or not their statutes have CA provisions. It is true that the number of license applications rejected as a proportion of the total number of such applications made to the regulatory agency may measure the stringency of application of the CA provision. However, even this measure is likely to be grossly misleading. In those states in which CA restrictions are strictly enforced, prospective applicants may not bother to file less promising applications. For those reasons, no attempt has been made to evaluate the impact of the CA provisions in the New York Statute.

CHAPTER 5

Regulation and the Characteristics of Loans and Borrowers

This chapter deals with the effects that rate ceilings and loan limits have on loan sizes, loan prices, and the risk category of borrowers who obtain credit in the New York consumer finance industry.

Loan Characteristics

LOAN SIZES

Loan Limits and Loan Sizes. The average sizes of loans made in New York as well as other states are largely determined by the levels of the prevailing loan limits. At first glance this proposition may seem entirely obvious. Actually, it holds only if the limits are restrictive in practice. If loan limits were set high enough so that all, or nearly all, loans that were demanded could be made, these loan limits would not perceptibly affect the average sizes of loans made. In practice, loan limits have a marked impact on the average sizes of loans made. Three pieces of evidence support this conclusion.

TABLE 3
Regulation and Some Characteristics of Loans

Equation	States[a]	Dependent Variable	Constant Term	Independent Variables, Coefficients, and Standard Errors		R^2
5-1	33	X_6	74.30	6.73 X_1[b] (2.20)	14.37 X_7[b] (6.27)	0.41

NOTE: X_1 = the loan limit (in hundreds of dollars); X_6 = the average size of loan made (in dollars); and X_7 = the per capita income of the state (in hundreds of dollars).

[a] The state is the unit of observation.

[b] Indicates significance of the coefficient at the 0.05 level.

First, as may be seen from Equation 5-1 of Table 3, states that have high loan limits tend to have large average loan sizes, although the relationship is by no means perfect. Second, as shown in Chart 2, the average size of loan made in New York State rose relatively steadily between 1946 and 1965, with the largest changes in growth rate of the average loan size occurring in 1949 and 1960, the years in which loan limits were raised. Third, the data on the size distribution of loans made in New York State between 1936 and 1965, given in Appendix D, exhibit the following pattern. In each case, as the loan limit was raised, the concentration of loans in the size group that was the highest prior to the increase in the loan limit gradually declined and loans became concentrated in the loan size group closest to the new loan limit. This gave the effect of a "pressure" gradually building up against the loan limit and being (temporarily) released by the increase in the loan limit.

Loan Limits, Price Levels, and Real Incomes. The loan limit is not the only determinant of the average size of loan made. It merely sets an upper limit that is more or less restrictive depending on its specific level. The average size of loan made in a state is also determined by the sizes of loans demanded and supplied at the given ceiling rates of charge. The sizes of loans demanded would be expected to increase as price levels rise since a greater dollar amount would be required to purchase the same goods and services. This relationship is in fact borne out by the trends in the average loan sizes and the consumer price index for New York City (given in Chart 2).

In its 1958 rate study, the New York State Banking Department found that the average loan size was larger for higher income borrowers than for borrowers in lower income classes.[1] This finding of a positive relationship between per capita real income and loan size is supported by the interstate comparisons of per capita income and average loan sizes for 1964 given in Equation 5-1. It is shown in Equation 5-1 that the level of per capita income is a significant determinant of the average size of loans made in a state, even after the impact of loan limits on loan sizes has been taken into account.

That loans demanded are larger the higher the price levels and real incomes suggests that there should be regular adjustments in loan limits to reflect movements in the price level and changes in borrowers' incomes if consumer finance companies are to accommo-

[1] The New York State Banking Department, *An Analysis of the Licensed Lenders Industry*, New York, 1958, p. 13.

CHART 2

Average Loan Size and Consumer Price Index, New York State, 1946-65

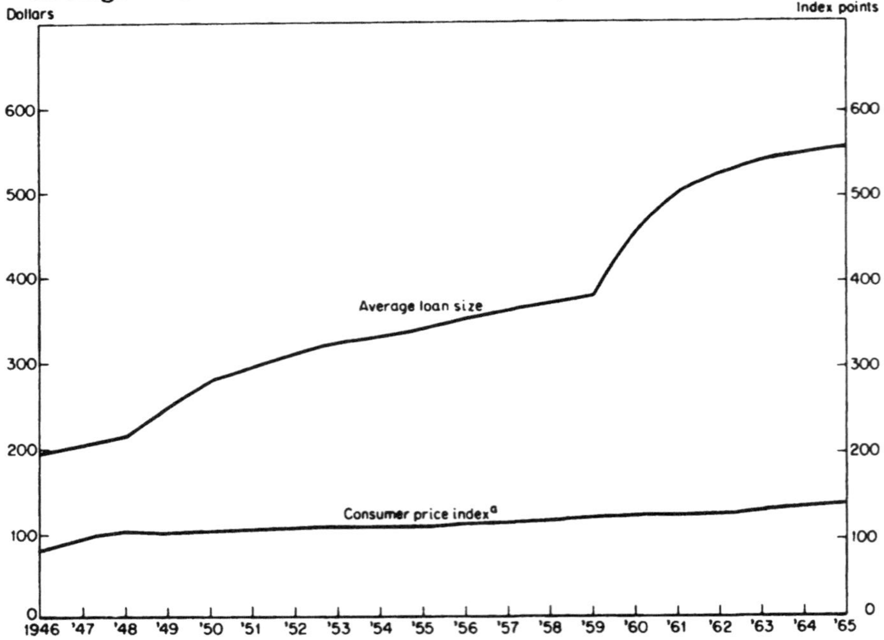

SOURCE: Computed from New York State Consumer Finance Association, *Statistical Information on All Licensed Lenders in New York State*, 1965; Bureau of the Census, *Statistical Abstract of the United States*, 1949-66; and Department of Labor, Bureau of Labor Statistics, *Monthly Labor Review*, 1948-66.

[a] Index for New York City only.

CHART 3

Erosion of the Purchasing Power of the New York Loan Limit, 1932-65
(1949 = 100)

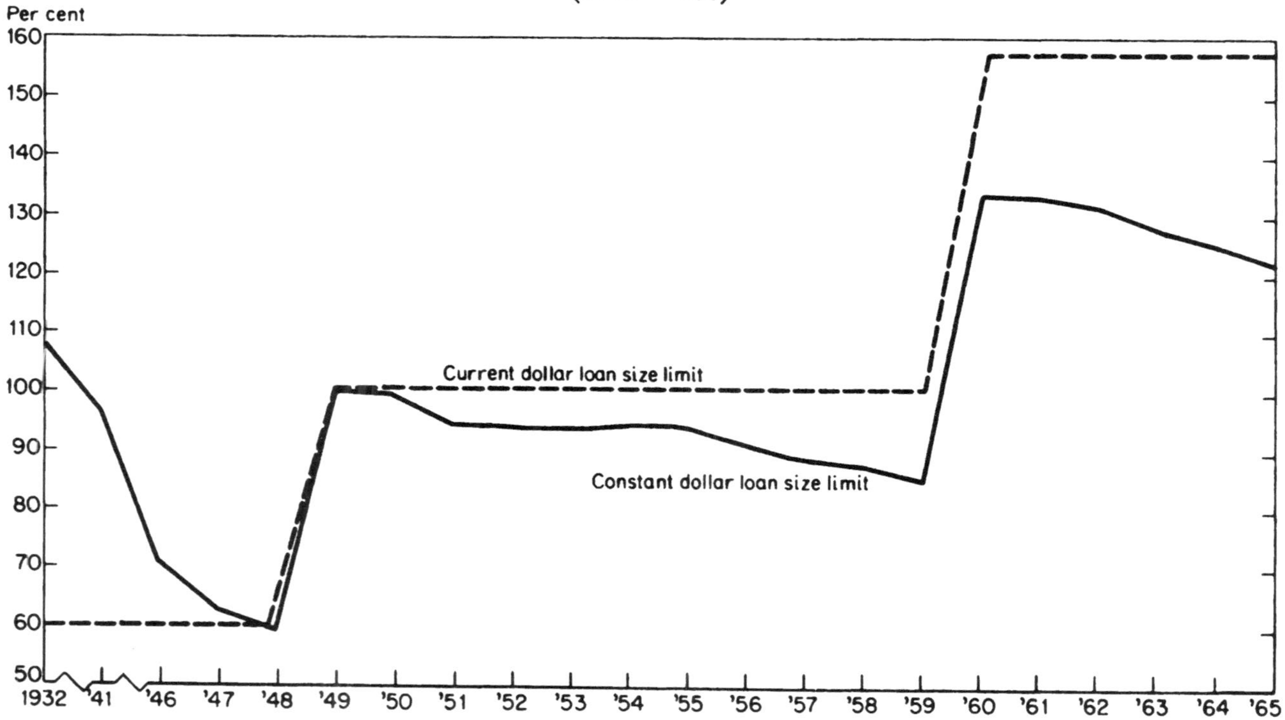

SOURCE: Same as Chart 2.

CHART 4

Constant Dollar Maximum Loan Size Limit of Consumer Finance Companies as a Percentage of Consumers' Real Annual Incomes, New York State, 1932-65

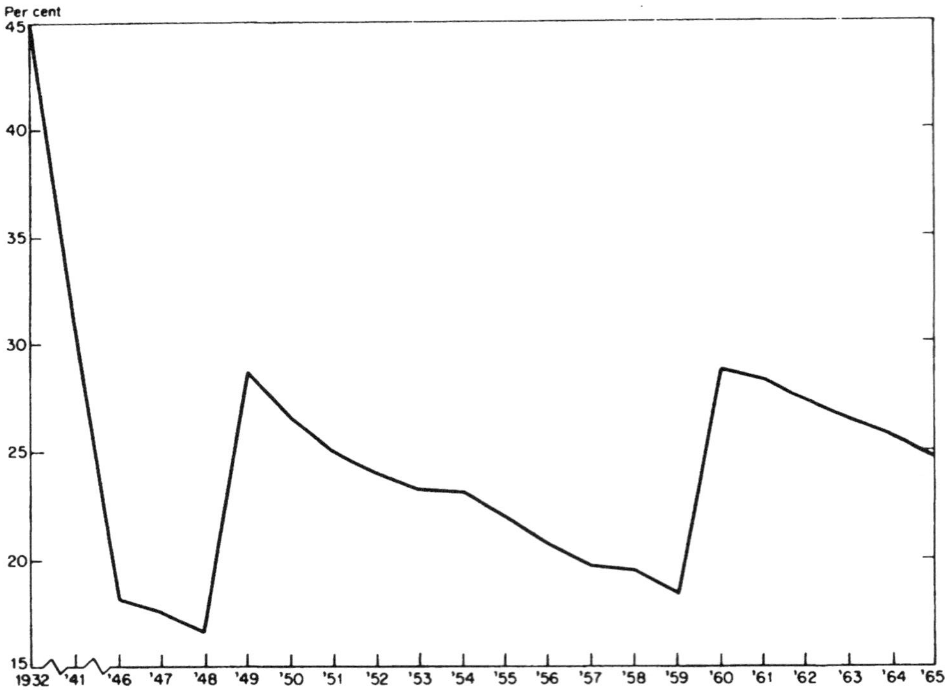

SOURCE: Same as Chart 2.

date the same classes of loans and groups of borrowers over time.

Chart 3 depicts changes in the purchasing power of the loan limit of the New York State consumer finance industry. Chart 4 shows the relationship between the loan limit and per capita real income for New York State. Both charts cover the 1932-65 period and demonstrate that the erosion of the purchasing power of the loan limit and its adequacy in terms of consumers' per capita real incomes began in each case immediately after it was established and continued quite steadily throughout its life. Because loan limits in New York were raised only twice in this 33-year period, there was a significant erosion of the purchasing power of the loan limit and its adequacy in terms of per capita real incomes in the intervals between loan limit increases. A large number of states have also had inflexible loan limits over relatively long periods (as shown in Chapter 4) and have experienced rising price levels and real incomes. Like New York, they have suffered erosion of the adequacy of their loan limits in terms of price levels and consumer incomes.

RELATIONSHIPS BETWEEN LEGAL RATES, LOAN LIMITS, AND AVERAGE LOAN SIZES

It was shown in Chapter 4 [2] that, compared to other states, New York has low rate ceilings on loans ranging from $100-$800 (the range studied). Appendix Table C-1 shows that the average gross income earned in New York is lower than that in the thirty-three other states for which data are available. The table also shows that New York has an average loan size of $544.37, higher than that of twenty-one states and lower than that of twelve states. Thus, although New York has a relatively low loan limit (twenty-four states are higher, seventeen are lower, and three are the same) that tends to reduce the average loan size, it has a relatively large average loan size. This relatively large loan size is probably explainable by adaptations of New York lenders to the prevailing (low) rate ceilings. This conclusion is based upon the following reasoning.

The demand of consumers for loans from the consumer finance industry is relatively unresponsive to the rate charged.[3] Thus any

[2] See Chart 1, particularly Part H.

[3] See F. Thomas Juster and Robert P. Shay, *Consumer Sensitivity to Finance Rates*, New York, National Bureau of Economic Research, 1964, *passim*.

significant differences that are found in the average sizes of loans made in high and low rate states would probably be the result of the responsiveness of lenders and not borrowers to the level of the regulated rate.

As noted in Chapter 4, because of the graduation of rate ceilings, as the size of loan increases in a state the average legal rate (and hence the average actual rate) declines. This inverse relationship between the size of loan and the permitted legal rate is a consequence only of the graduated pattern of rate ceilings within states and the virtually universal practice in the industry of charging the maximum allowable rate. It need not hold among states. For example, if, in State A, the average legal rate on a $300 loan is 2 per cent whereas in State B the average legal rate on a $400 loan is 3 per cent, the opposite relationship between average legal rate and loan size would be found to hold among states as holds within states. That is to say, there would be a direct and not an inverse relationship between loan sizes and average rates.

Chart 5 shows the relationships between the average rate charged [4] and the average loan size for thirty-three states. As may be seen from this chart, and Equation 5-2 of Table 4, there is a significant inverse correlation between the average rate charged and the average size of loan made. Thus the relationship between legal rates and loan sizes which holds within states (because of the graduated rate structure) also holds among states. As is widely believed and supported by Equation 5-3 of Table 4, larger loans are significantly cheaper (per dollar) to make than are smaller loans. Thus the observed inverse relationship between average rates and average loan sizes probably represents an adjustment by lenders to favor those loan sizes that are more profitable in relation to operating expenses. This conclusion is particularly compelling when it is recalled that there is nothing in the national pattern of regulation outlined in Chapter 4 which would make inevitable the inverse correlation between average rates and average loan sizes.

[4] The measure of gross average rate that is used here and in the rest of the study comprises the gross income of consumer finance companies from all sources related to their operations under the small loan laws outlined in Appendix B. Revenues from insurance, default and extension charges, recording fees, etc. are included. This measure of gross income is thus more comprehensive than the "interest or charges earned" item which appears in the state supervisors' reports as a subcategory of the gross income measures used here. However, "interest charges" are by far the largest component of total gross income. Thus the results of the analysis would not be significantly altered if interest charges were substituted for the more comprehensive measure of gross income.

CHART 5

Relationship Between Average Loan Size and Gross Annual Rate, 1964

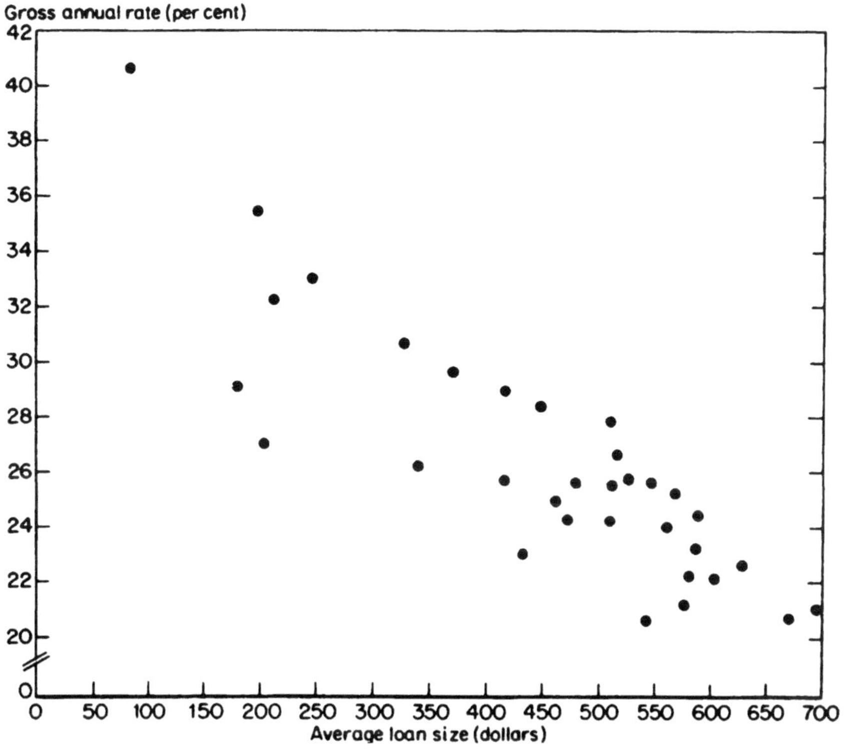

SOURCE: Computed from reports of State Supervisors.

TABLE 4

Regulation and Some Characteristics of Loans

Equation	States[a]	Dependent Variable	Constant Term	Independent Variables, Coefficients, and Standard Errors	R^2
5-2	33	X_6	1254.71	$-30.29\ X_8$[b] (3.39)	0.72
5-3	15	X_9	31.67	$-\ 0.04\ X_6$[b] (0.002)	0.76

NOTE: X_6 = the average size of loan made (in dollars); X_8 = the average gross annual rate charged by all lenders in a state (in per cent); and X_9 = the operating expenses (i.e., all expenses excluding only the interest paid and state and federal income taxes) as a percentage of average loans outstanding.

[a] The state is the unit of observation.

[b] Indicates significance of the coefficient at the 0.05 level.

The conclusion that lenders adjust their loan offerings so as to make small loans where the rate ceiling is high and large loans where the rate ceiling is low is supported by casual observation of the advertisements of some lenders. For example, in states where the rates on very small loans are thought to be such as to make these loans unprofitable, lenders may place lower limits of $25 or $50 on their loans. Similarly, where the rate on large loans is judged to be lower than the cost of supplying them, lenders may place an upper limit that is lower than the statutory loan limit on the sizes of loans they offer (for example, in California many lenders advertise loans of up to $2,500 only although the loan limit is $5,000).

TRENDS IN AVERAGE RATES CHARGED

Chart 6 depicts movements in the average rate charged in New York State between 1936 and 1965. There is a marked long-term down trend due to the increasing sizes of loans made and the inverse relationship between loan size and rate.[5]

[5] The increase in the average rate charged between 1943 and 1945 is due to the sharp drop in loans outstanding in these years and the procedure used in computing average rates (which was to compute these as a percentage of average loan balances outstanding at year end). The increase in the average rate in the 1960-61 period resulted from the increase in the legal rate on loans above $300, which became effective July 1, 1960.

CHART 6

Total Operating Income as a Percentage of Outstanding Loans, New York, 1936-65

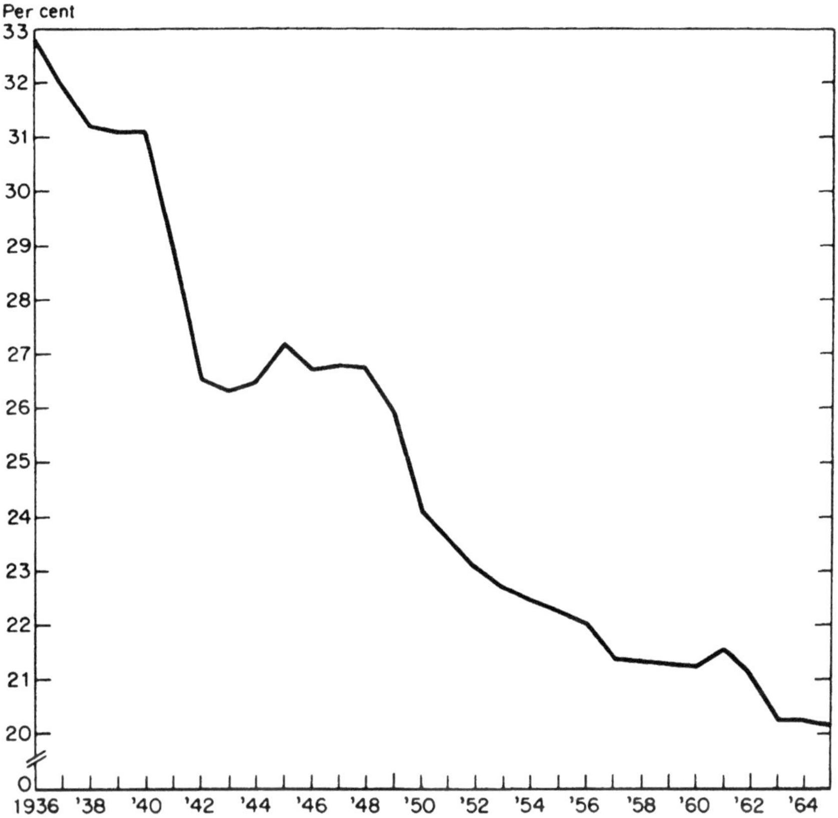

SOURCE: New York State Consumer Finance Association, *Statistical Information on All Licensed Lenders in New York State,* 1965.

The persistent decline of average rates is inevitable given a static rate structure, the practice of charging ceiling rates, and the continual increases in average loan sizes. Further, the general practice of maintaining rates unchanged on lower loan size brackets and increasing only the loan limit on the highest loan bracket (see Chapter 4) does not solve this problem and may only aggravate it. If desired, average rates can be maintained unchanged in a multiple bracket rate structure only by rate increases or by changing the sizes of each loan bracket so that the same percentage of loans is made in each bracket and hence at each rate.[6]

The same principles that explain the decline in average rates as the average loan size grows also operate to decrease the average rate on constant dollar loans. As price levels rise, an increasing dollar amount is required to maintain purchasing power constant. This increased dollar amount bears a lower rate because a larger part of the larger loan is in a higher loan size bracket (which bears a lower rate).

Borrower Risk

For the purposes of this study, risk has been measured by the ratio of the balance sheet item reserve for bad debts to the dollar value of loans outstanding. It is recognized that this is an imperfect measure of risk. Loss rates and hence reserves for bad debts (which reflect the history of loss experience) may be the same in states in which risk differs greatly if the expenditures on screening loan applications and on collections for example, differ greatly among these states. However, no satisfactory measure of expenses incurred to minimize losses could be developed. Classifications in state supervisors' reports such as "collection expenses" are largely arbitrary. In a sense, almost every cost of conducting a small loan business may be meaningfully considered at least in part a cost of reducing risk.

Assuming that average costs are just covered by average revenues, as would be the case in a purely competitive market over the long run, higher rates would be required to permit lenders to accommodate higher risk borrowers. The reason is that there are greater losses and

[6] For a fuller treatment of these procedures see my "On the Inflexibility of Small Loan Rate and Loan Size Ceilings," *Personal Finance Law Quarterly Report*, Vol. 19, No. 2, Spring 1965, pp. 57-60.

TABLE 5

Regulation and the Characteristics of Borrowers

Equation	States[a]	Dependent Variable	Constant Term	Independent Variables, Coefficients, and Standard Errors					R^2
5-4	15	X_9	10.31	$2.02\,X_{10}$[b] (0.88)					0.29
5-5	26	X_{10}	0.21	$0.12\,X_8$[b] (0.04)					0.24
5-6	18	X_{10}	−6.79	$0.18\,X_8$[b] (0.06)	$0.16\,X_{11}$ (0.16)	$0.23\,X_7$ (0.11)	$0.26\,X_{12}$ (0.19)	$0.18\,X_{13}$ (0.17)	0.55

NOTE: X_7 = the per capita income of the state (in hundreds of dollars); X_8 = the average gross annual rate charged by all lenders in the state (in per cent); X_9 = the operating expenses (i.e., all expenses excluding only the interest paid and state and federal income taxes) as a percentage of average loans outstanding; X_{10} = reserve for bad debts as a percentage of average loans outstanding in 1964; X_{11} = the number of finance companies' loan branches per 1,000 households; X_{12} = the number of credit unions per 1,000 households; and X_{13} = the number of commercial bank branches per 1,000 households. For equations in this table, X_9 excludes provisions for losses.

[a] The state is the unit of observation.

[b] Indicates significance of the coefficient at the 0.05 level.

other costs of lending to and collecting from a riskier class of borrowers (Equation 5-4 of Table 5).[7]

However, there is no necessary correlation between rate and risk in a noncompetitive market. Without extending riskier loans, lenders may charge higher rates where the rate ceilings are higher and thus increase their profit. It is important to recognize that such a practice need not result from any conscious effort on the part of lenders to earn higher returns in states where rates are higher. It could result from simple rigidities or imperfections in the loan market. For example, national chains generally provide their branch office employees in all states with standardized instructions for accepting or rejecting loan applicants and this tends to equalize the average risk accommodated in high and low rate states.

New York's reserve for bad debts was 2.89 per cent of small loans receivable (for 1964). Eighteen states had higher reserves for bad debts relative to receivables and seven had lower reserves for bad debts relative to receivables. To test whether New York's relatively low ranking with respect to bad debt reserves is related to its low ranking based upon average income, an investigation was made of the risk-rate relationship for all states for which data were available in 1964.

Chart 7 and Equation 5-5 of Table 5 reveal the finding of a significant positive relationship between risk, as measured here, and rate. Equation 5-6 of Table 5 introduces two other classes of factors, the per capita income of the state and the degree of competition in the loan market, and shows that rate has a significant positive effect on risk even after the impact of these factors on risk has been taken into account. These findings suggest that the observation that New York lenders do not serve a highly risky class of borrowers (relative to the lenders in other states) may be explained at least partly by New York's relatively low rates.

Further, a priori analysis and the available data suggest that it is New York's low rates and not its low loan limit that lead to the low average risk of customers served in New York. Small loans would be expected to be higher risk on theoretical grounds. The risk-rate relationship for the states for which data were available confirmed this expectation, as noted earlier, by showing a significant positive correlation between rate and risk.

[7] There is an identification problem resulting from correlating losses with costs of lending when the costs of lending include bad debt expenses. However, this problem is not serious. See John M. Chapman and Robert P. Shay, editors, *The Consumer Finance Industry—Its Costs and Regulation*, New York, 1967, p. 66.

CHART 7

Relationship Between Ratio of Reserve for Bad Debts to Average Loans Outstanding and Gross Annual Rate, 1964 (per cent)

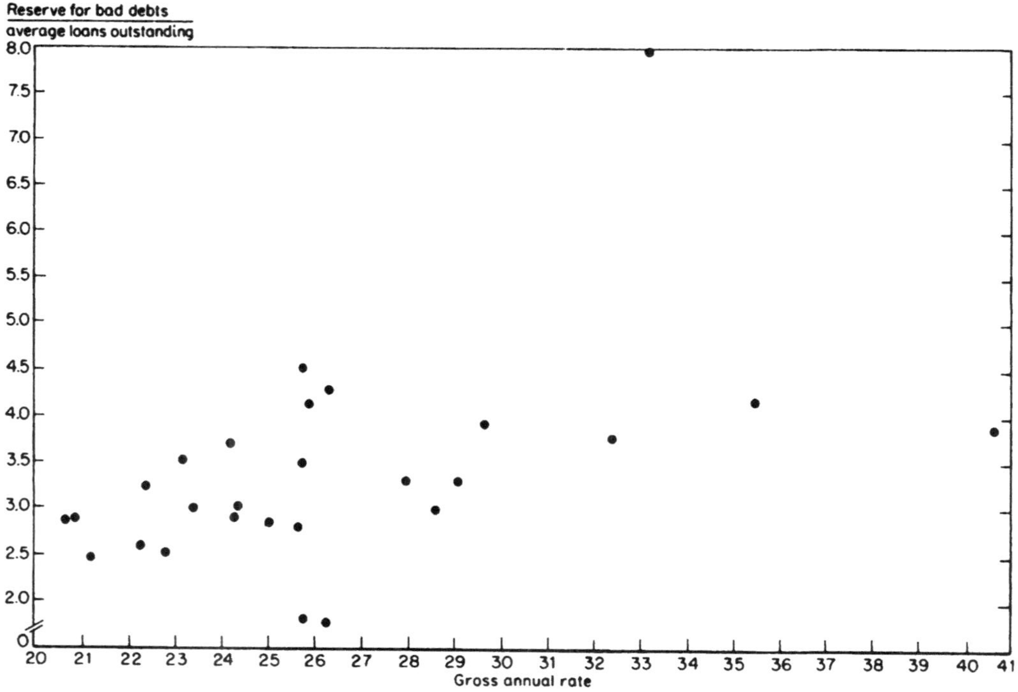

SOURCE: Computed from reports of State Supervisors.

Since rates and loan sizes are negatively correlated and loan sizes and loan limits are also negatively correlated, the typical risk-loan limit relationship would also be expected to be negative. However, New York has a relatively low average rate and relatively low loan limit. As shown further, the average risk of customers served in New York is relatively low. It may therefore be concluded that New York's low rates (and not its low loan limit) are the dominant determinant of the low average risk of customers served in New York.

CHAPTER 6

Regulation and the Amount of Lending Facilities

This chapter deals with the effects of rate ceilings and loan limits on the quantity of lending facilities that are supplied by the consumer finance industry in New York State. Four measures of the volume of lending facilities are used. These are the number of lenders and loan branches [1] and the number and dollar amount of loans extended.

The Number of Lenders and Loan Branches

THE NUMBER OF LENDERS

Of all states for which data are available, New York has the lowest average gross income per dollar of loans outstanding (see Appendix C). New York also has the fewest lenders per thousand households. That the relative fewness of lenders in New York is due to the relatively low rates charged in New York seems probable. The evidence and reasons follow.

First, Chart 8 shows the relationship between average gross annual rate and the number of lenders per thousand households. The number of lenders is reduced to a per thousand household basis to eliminate differences due to the sheer size of states. Chart 8 and the supporting Equation 6-1 of Table 6 demonstrate that there is a significant positive relationship between the number of lenders per thousand households and the average rate. Equation 6-2 is designed to show the impact of rate on the number of lenders after the effects of credit union and bank competition as well as population growth are taken into account. It indicates that the positive correlation between rate and

[1] As used here, a "lender" is a lending firm that may have one or more lending outlets or "loan branches."

CHART 8

Relationship Between Number of Lenders per Thousand Households and Gross Annual Rate, 1964

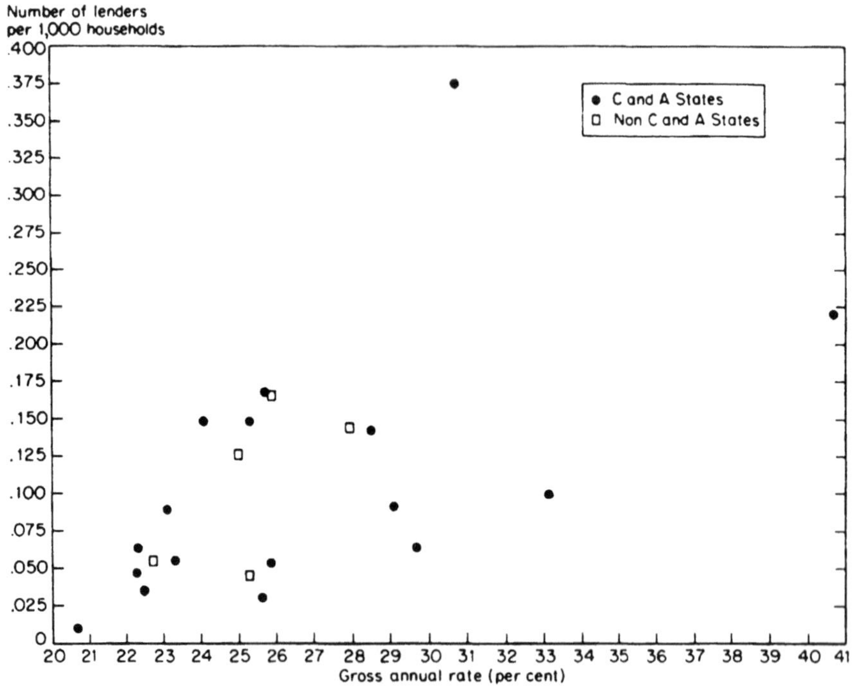

SOURCE: Computed from reports of State Supervisors.

TABLE 6

Regulation and the Number and Sizes of Lenders

Equation	States[a]	Dependent Variable	Constant Term	Independent Variables, Coefficients, and Standard Errors				R^2
6-1	22	X_{14}	–0.17	$0.01\ X_8$[b] (0.002)				0.32
6-2	12	X_{14}	–2.84	$0.13\ X_8$ (0.06)	$0.11\ X_{12}$ (0.20)	$-0.01\ X_{13}$ (0.28)	$0.99\ X_{15}$ (1.46)	0.39
6-3	18	X_9	22.85	$-0.36\ X_{16}$[b] (0.10)				0.42
6-4	22	X_{17}	8.48	$-0.17\ X_8$[b] (0.07)				0.21
6-5	21	X_{16}	78.92	$-2.28\ X_8$[b] (0.83)				0.29

NOTE: X_8 = the average gross annual rate charged by all lenders in the state (in per cent); X_9 = the operating expenses (i.e., all expenses excluding only the interest paid and state and federal income taxes) as a percentage of average loans outstanding; X_{12} = the number of credit unions per 1,000 households; X_{13} = the number of commercial bank branches per 1,000 households; X_{14} = the number of finance company lenders per 1,000 households; X_{15} = the average simple annual growth rate of the state's population over the 1960-64 period (in per cent); X_{16} = the loans made per lender (in hundreds of thousands of dollars); and X_{17} = the number of loan branches per lender.

[a] The state is the unit of observation.

[b] Indicates significance of the coefficient at the 0.05 level.

lender population still holds when these other factors are taken into account but its significance is considerably reduced.

The relationships in Chart 8 and Equations 6-1 and 6-2 of Table 6 demonstrate that the number of lenders per thousand households increases systematically with the level of average rates. The reason for this positive relationship between rate and the number of lenders per thousand households may be that there are important cost differences among lenders. Specifically, if there are major cost differences among lenders, and if the relationship between lenders' costs and rates are such that not all lenders earn profits above competitive levels, the number of lenders would tend to be lower relative to population in low rate states.[2]

To establish whether there are in fact cost differences among lenders and to ascertain their nature, further analysis was conducted. This analysis revealed a significant inverse correlation between lender size and operating expenses per dollar of loans outstanding (Equation 6-3 of Table 6), i.e., the larger the average size of lender in a state, the lower the operating expenses per dollar of loans outstanding.

This would suggest that low rate states would typically have large lenders. A comparative analysis of the average size of lenders in New York was made. It was found that when lender size was measured by number of offices per lender, New York had the largest average lender size of the twenty-six states for which data are available. When lender size was measured by the dollar value of loans made per lender, New York also had the largest average lender size of the twenty-two states for which data are available. To ascertain whether the relationship between rate and lender size established for New York is typical, further tests were carried out.

First, an analysis was made of the relationship between rate and the number of offices per lender in different states. If large lenders are lower cost than small ones as suggested by Equation 6-3, the number of offices per lender should be inversely correlated with average rate. The result of the test is given in Equation 6-4 of Table 6. It indicates that the number of offices per lender is significantly higher in low rate states. This finding is buttressed by the time series data on New York State for the period 1932-65 (presented in Appendix E), which show that the number of loan branches per lender

[2] The reason is, of course, that the lower the permissible rate, the fewer the number of lenders who can operate profitably. However, if all lenders would otherwise earn profits above competitive levels, lowered rates may not cause them to exit, but merely reduce their earnings rates.

has been growing steadily as average rate has been falling Chart 6).[3] It is also supported by the significant inverse correlation (see Equation 6-5) between average gross rate charged and lender size as measured by the dollar value of loans made per lender.

It is not possible to determine from the available data whether the lower cost of larger lenders is due to their greater efficiency or to the larger average loans made by these larger lenders in low rate states. The findings demonstrate only that larger lenders have lower average costs. They provide no insight into the reasons for this cost difference.

To sum up, the fewness of lenders in New York is probably due to the low average rate in New York. Also, the larger average size of New York lenders can probably be explained by the cost advantage of larger lenders which permits them to survive in low rate states such as New York.

NUMBER OF LOAN BRANCHES

New York has fewer loan offices per thousand households than has any of the other states for which data are available. In an effort to ascertain whether New York's low ranking on the basis of branch office population was related to its low rate, the relationship between average rate charged and the number of loan offices per thousand households was studied for all states for which data are available. Equations 6-6 and 6-7 of Table 7 show that while the relationship between rate and number of loan branches is positive it is not significant either when the effect of average rate alone is studied (Equation 6-6) or when the impact of competition and population growth rate have been allowed for (Equation 6-7).

One possible explanation of this lack of significant relationship between rate and the number of branch offices is that the high loan limits of low rate states make the potential dollar volume of loan business in these states larger, thereby attracting loan branches in spite of the low rate. New York has few loan branches because New York has a relatively low loan limit coupled with its low rate ceiling.

[3] The increasing share of consumer finance companies' loans outstanding in New York accounted for by chains is further evidence in support of the finding that chains are more lower cost than independents. See Michael Kawaja, "Regulation of the New York State Consumer Finance Industry," unpublished Ph.D. dissertation, Columbia University, 1964, p. 100.

TABLE 7

Regulation and the Number and Sizes of Loan Branches

Equation	States[a]	Dependent Variable	Constant Term	Independent Variables, Coefficients, and Standard Errors				R^2
6-6	34	X_{11}	0.7	0.01 X_8 (0.01)				0.06
6-7	22	X_{11}	3.28	0.14 X_8 (0.11)	−0.14 X_{12} (0.35)	−0.23 X_{13} (0.35)	−0.37 X_{15} (0.33)	0.23
6-8	33	X_{18}	11.82	−0.30 X_8[b] (0.07)				0.37
6-9	29	X_9	22.71	−1.45 X_{18}[b] (0.34)				0.40

NOTE: X_8 = the average gross annual rate charged by all lenders in the state (in per cent); X_9 = the operating expenses (i.e., all expenses excluding only the interest paid and state and federal income taxes) as a percentage of average loans outstanding; X_{11} = the number of finance companies' loan branches per 1,000 households; X_{12} = the number of credit unions per 1,000 households; X_{13} = the number of commercial banks per 1,000 households; X_{15} = the average simple annual growth rate of the state's population over the 1960-64 period (in per cent); X_{18} = the loans made per loan branch (in hundreds of thousands of dollars).

[a] The state is the unit of observation.

[b] Indicates significance of the coefficient at the 0.05 level.

This would suggest that the potential loan volume in New York would be low and hence able to attract and support only relatively few loan branches as observed here.

In addition to the impact of the rate level on branch office population, the effect of the rate level on average office size was studied. Equation 6-8 (Table 7) shows that there is a significant inverse correlation between average rate and average office size (as measured by the dollar amount of loans made per branch office). The probable explanation of this relationship between rate and office size is that larger offices are lower cost (as shown in Equation 6-9 of Table 7). Thus larger offices predominate (since they are the only ones that can be operated profitably) in the lower rate states. For example, New York, which is relatively a very low rate state, has the largest average office size of the thirty-five states for which data are available.

It is worth noting that the data cannot demonstrate conclusively that there are economies of scale for lenders and that large loan branches have lower unit costs than do small offices. (However, they are consistent with such a theory.) Because low average rates are associated with large loans, the different concentrations of lenders in high and low rate states and the greater average size of lenders and offices in low rate states may possibly result from differences in loan sizes (due either to demand or loan limits) and not average rates.

The Number and Amount of Loans Made

THE NUMBER OF LOANS

New York, a relatively low rate state, has relatively few loans per thousand households. Specifically, New York has the lowest average rate of all states for which data are available and has fewer loans per thousand households than twenty-nine states and more loans per thousand households than only five states. Equation 6-10 of Table 8 demonstrates a systematic positive relationship between the level of the average rate charged and the number of loans made per thousand households when all states for which data are available are considered. However, as in most of the analysis up to this point, it is difficult to separate the effects of rate ceilings from those of loan limits, since low average rates are associated with large loans.

It is probable that the level of the rate charged by itself would tend to affect the number of loans made. Where the rate is low, as in New

TABLE 8

Regulation and the Number and Dollar Amount of Loans Made

Equation	States[a]	Dependent Variable	Constant Term	Independent Variables, Coefficients, and Standard Errors			R^2
6-10	33	X_{19}	–395.38	27.69 X_8[b] (8.49)			0.26
6-11	31	X_{20}	684.28	–10.44 X_8[b] (3.23)	–14.92 X_7[b] (4.32)	28.92 X_{15}[b] (8.91)	0.38

NOTE: X_7 = the per capita income of the state (in hundreds of dollars); X_8 = the average gross annual rate charged by all lenders in the state (in per cent); X_{15} = the average simple annual growth rate of the state's population over the 1960-64 period (in per cent); X_{19} = the number of loans made per 1,000 households; and X_{20} = the dollar value of loans made per 1,000 households (in thousands of dollars).

[a] The state is the unit of observation.

[b] Indicates significance of the coefficient at the 0.05 level.

York, fewer higher cost loans can be made. Because of the relative unresponsiveness of borrowers to the rate level, the lower rates may not attract offsetting numbers of borrowers.

Another probable explanation of the smaller number of loans made in states with lower average charges is that these states have relatively high loan limits. At first glance it may be expected that the number of loans made would be larger in states with high loan limits. This may be expected since in the states with high loan limits all the loans that can be made in low loan limit states can still be made. In addition, larger loans that could not be made if the loan limit were lower would also be made. However, when borrowers need loans that are larger than the permitted loan limit, some simply "double up" or make several loans from different lenders, which total to the sum they wish to borrow.

For example, if the loan limit is $300, but a consumer wishes to borrow $800, he may make three different loans ($300, $300, and $200). Actually, there is probably a tendency to make fewer than the three loans because of the greater cost (including inconvenience) of making three loans as opposed to one. The consumer may thus make only two loans, of, say, $300 each, thereby foregoing $200. Thus, whereas only one loan would have been made if the loan limit were $800, three or perhaps two loans are made if the loan limit is $300. A time series analysis of the number of loans made in New York State (presented in Appendix F) supports the finding that the number of loans falls markedly when the loan limit is raised.

In light of the above analysis it may be concluded that New York has relatively few loans primarily because of its low rate. If New York's relatively low loan limit were dominant, it would have led to relatively many loans being made in New York.

It is worth noting that the effect of low loan limits in increasing the number of loans is undesirable. Smaller loans are higher cost and bear higher charges than larger loans. The borrower who has to make three loans instead of one because of the restrictive loan limit therefore pays a higher price than he otherwise would. Also, assuming free and rational consumer choice, the forcing of the alternative of borrowing less (i.e., say $600 as opposed to $800) is undesirable.

THE AMOUNT OF LOANS

The dollar value of loans made per thousand households in New York is lower than that in 26 other states and higher than the dollar value of loans per thousand households made in eight states. However, the correlation between New York's low ranking on the basis of average gross income and its low ranking on the basis of the dollar amount of loans made is not typical. Equation 6-11 of Table 8 shows that there is a significant inverse relationship between the average rate and the dollar amount of loans made when all states for which data are available are considered. That is to say, there is a systematic tendency for the dollar value of loans made to be higher in low rate states. Equation 6-11 reduces the value of loans made to a per thousand household basis and thus eliminates differences among states due to their population. It also eliminates differences among states based upon the levels of their per capita personal incomes and their population growth rates.

Thus, whereas Equation 6-10 demonstrates that a smaller number of loans is made in relatively low rate states, Equation 6-11 indicates that a larger dollar amount of loans is typically made in these states (New York being, as noted, an exception). This phenomenon may be explained as follows.

Low average rates are typically associated with high loan limits. Even if the level of the average rate charged affects the number of loans made, then probably the larger loan sizes in low rate states (which is a consequence of their less restrictive loan limits and low rates) more than offsets their smaller number. Thus, although the consumer may make a larger number of loans when the loan limit is low, he may borrow less in dollar amount. The importance and nature of the effect of the loan limit on the amount of loans made is further illustrated by the experience in New York where only the loan limit changed in 1949 and the amount of loans expanded dramatically (Appendix E).

This analysis of the positive correlation between rate and number of loans and the inverse relationship between rate and amount of loans sheds light on the New York industry. New York, a low rate state, would be expected to have, as it does, relatively few loans. However, if New York were typical, it would have a high loan limit associated with its low rate and this would be expected to lead to the supply of a large amount of loans in New York in spite of its low rate. However, New York is not typical in that it has a relatively low loan limit as well as a relatively low average rate. Both low rates and low loan limits tend to reduce the amount of loans made and explain New York's low ranking on the basis of the dollar amount of loans made relative to population.

CHAPTER 7

Regulation and Earnings

This chapter deals with the effects of rate ceilings and loan limits on the consumer finance industry's earnings at one point in time, 1964, and the effects of a decline in gross rate on the New York industry's earnings over time.

Regulation and Earnings

There was a wide range of earnings rates among the states in 1964. Earnings rates were measured as net income (after all expenses but before interest and taxes) as a percentage of average loans outstanding.[1] Of the thirty-five states for which data were available, net earnings ranged from 7.5 to 11.8 per cent for all but three states. The three states outside this range were Oklahoma, which had net earnings of 3.3 per cent, Wisconsin, 4.9 per cent, and West Virginia, 13.3 per cent.

New York, as shown earlier, had the lowest average gross rate of all states for which data are available. However, average net earnings rates in New York are higher than in twenty-two other states and lower than average net earnings rates in twelve other states. In an effort to ascertain the reasons for the difference in New York's rankings on the basis of gross and net income, an analysis was made of the gross-income – net-income relationship for all states for which data were available. The results are shown in Chart 9 and Equation 7-1 of Table 9.

[1] It was not possible to compute net earnings after taxes and interest as a percentage of equity. Interest paid by lenders as reported to state supervisors are largely interoffice transactions (between subsidiaries and their parent companies). Interest rates paid, the amount of borrowings, and the amount of equity capital are largely determined by the convenience of the parent company. They cannot be taken as indicating either the ultimate source of funds or the rates of interest that would have to be paid to outside suppliers of capital.

CHART 9

Relationship Between Gross and Net Income, 1964

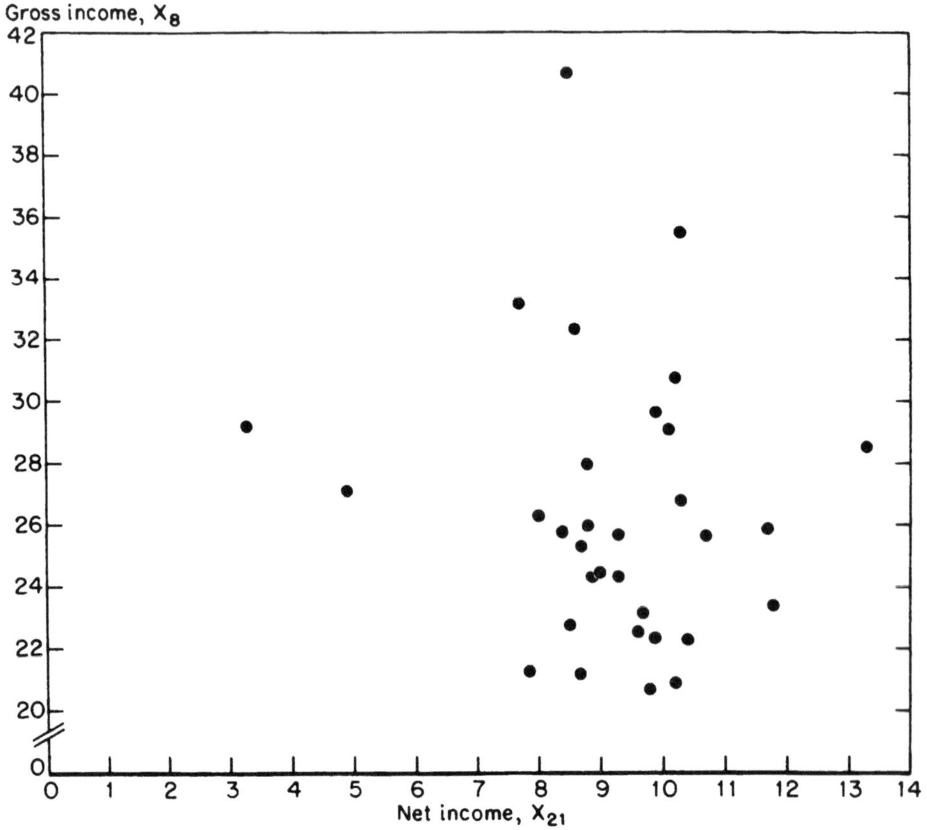

TABLE 9
Regulation and Earnings

Equation	States[a]	Dependent Variable	Constant Term	Independent Variables, Coefficients, and Standard Errors	R^2
7-1	32	X_{21}	9.81	$-0.02\ X_8$ (0.06)	0.00
7-2	31	X_9	–9.79	$1.01\ X_8$[b] (0.05)	0.93

NOTE: X_8 = the average gross annual rate charged by all lenders in the state (in per cent); X_9 = the operating expenses (i.e., all expenses excluding only the interest paid on state and federal income taxes) as a percentage of average loans outstanding; X_{21} = the average net annual earnings of consumer finance companies as a percentage of their average loans outstanding. Net earnings are computed as total gross income less all expenses, excluding income taxes (state and federal) and interest paid on borrowed funds.

[a] The state is the unit of observation.

[b] Indicates significance of the coefficient at the 0.05 level.

Equation 7-1 reveals that there is no systematic relationship between the level of the average gross rate in a state and the industry's average net earnings. This is explainable by cost differences among high and low rate states that probably result from the earlier noted adjustments of (1) loan sizes, (2) risk, and (3) the number and size of lenders and loan branches, to the level of the average rate.

The extent of these adjustments is indicated by the nearly perfect correlation between gross income and operating expenses per dollar of outstandings, when all states for which data are available are considered. As shown in Equation 7-2 of Table 9, the correlation is significant at the 0.001 level. Looking at New York separately, it is found that New York has a lower average gross income than all other states that were studied and also has a lower ratio of operating expenses to average loans outstanding than twenty-nine out of thirty states for which data are available. As shown in earlier chapters, the New York industry has adapted to its low gross rates by achieving operating economies through adjustments that result in the New York industry being characterized by relatively (1) large average loan sizes, (2) low average risk, and (3) few but large lenders and branch offices. It is these adjustments which permit the New York industry to rank thirteenth out of thirty-five states in net earnings on average outstandings in spite of its relatively low gross income.

Of course, these industry adjustments do not mean that any individual lender should not prefer higher rate states because the industry's net earnings may not be higher in these states. It means only that there is no systematic tendency for net operating earnings of all lenders to be higher or lower in these states. Any individual lender who does not experience all or any of these adjustments may do better in higher rate states. This may be particularly true, for example, of the lender whose forte is making the higher risk smaller loans that are characteristic of high rate states.

The lack of correlation between gross rate and net yield also does not mean that one should be indifferent to alternative rate structures. As emphasized up to this point, there are marked differences in the industry's characteristics in high and low rate states. One who seeks to have credit made available legally to the high risk borrower will prefer a high rate ceiling to a low one; one who seeks to encourage the small businessman to engage in the lending business will prefer a high rate to a low rate; and so on.

Regulation and Trends in Earnings

Table 10 shows the earnings and expenses of the New York consumer finance industry over the period 1936-65. Except for the higher levels attained in the period 1936-41, there is no discernible trend in net earnings before taxes (as a percentage of average loans outstanding).

However, in the 1936-65 period (and particularly in the 1941-65 period) gross earnings rates declined substantially and more in absolute and relative terms, as well as more persistently, than did net earnings. This finding buttresses the earlier finding, based on interstate comparisons, that there is no significant relationship between gross earnings and net earnings.

Further, over time the New York industry underwent many of the adjustments suggested in earlier chapters as the reasons for this lack of correlation between gross and net earnings. Specifically, as shown in Appendix D, the average size of loans made has increased persistently throughout the 1936-65 period as gross earnings declined. Also, as Table 10 shows there has been a long-term reduction in bad debt charges as a percentage of average loans outstanding. For example, in 1936-40, bad debt charges averaged 2.54 per cent of average loans outstanding and, in 1961-65, bad debt charges averaged 1.49 per cent of average loans outstanding. Finally, as shown in Table 10 and Appendix E, the average size of lenders and loan branches increased steadily as gross earnings declined.

TABLE 10

Selected Earnings and Expense Ratios, New York Consumer Finance Industry, 1936-1965 (Yearly Average)

	1936-40	1941-45	1946-50	1951-55	1956-60	1961-65
Average size of loan made (in dollars)	157.10	170.01	226.36	318.66	380.48	530.42
Average loans outstanding per office (in dollars)	190,400	196,200	303,000	471,800	551,000	712,600
Total operating income, as per cent of average outstanding loans	31.65	27.11	26.05	22.82	21.48	20.71
Items as a percentage of average loans outstanding						
Operating expenses:						
Advertising	2.48	1.98	1.54	.94	.83	.62
Rent	1.22	1.35	1.05	.81	.88	.77
Salaries	6.58	7.06	6.93	5.79	5.38	4.68
Supervision and administration	1.07	1.17	[a]	[a]	[a]	[a]
Other operating expense	3.84	3.89	3.75	3.75	3.04	2.66
Total operating expense	15.19	15.45	13.27	11.29	10.13	8.73
Net operating income	16.45	11.66	12.78	11.53	11.36	11.97
Net bad debt charges	2.54	1.32	1.12	1.36	1.43	1.49
Net before interest and taxes	13.90	10.34	11.67	10.17	9.93	10.48

Source: New York State Banking Department, *Annual Report of the Superintendent of Banks.*

[a] Items formerly reported as "Supervision and Administration" now allocated to specific expense items. Adjusted to 1945.

APPENDIX A

Loan Limits and Rate Ceilings of Credit Unions and Commercial Banks, New York State, 1964

The loan limits and maximum rates of charge for credit unions and commercial banks operating in New York State, unlike those for consumer finance companies, are a function not only of the size of the loan, but also such factors as the amount of paid-in capital and the purpose of the loan. Accordingly, these do not lend themselves easily to tabulation and have therefore been paraphrased from the relevant statutes. As of 1964, these regulatory limits were as follows:

Credit Unions. State and federal credit unions have the same rate ceilings. Credit unions are legally authorized to charge on any loan a rate not exceeding one per cent per month.[1]

State credit unions are permitted to make unsecured loans, net of the borrower's pledged shares, up to $500. Where the share capital of the credit union exceeds $100,000 and is not in excess of $250,000, loans on the same basis may not exceed $700. When the capital of the credit union is over $250,000, but not over $1 million, unsecured loans up to $1,200 may be made. On a secured basis, whenever capital is in excess of $500,000, loans may be made up to $5,000, net of the borrower's shares, except for certain real estate and guaranteed educational loans. The permissible limit for the net aggregate liability of any member is $10,000 net of the borrower's shares, for any credit union with capital in excess of $500,000.[2]

[1] *New York Banking Law* S453 (1962); Banks and Banking, Federal Credit Union Act, 12 U.S.C. S1757.

[2] The law governing New York State credit unions was changed in 1965 to permit state credit unions to make unsecured loans, net of the borrower's pledged shares up to $750 provided that such loans may not exceed 10 per cent of the share capital. Where the share capital of the credit union exceeds $1 million, unsecured loans up to $1,200 may be made. On a secured basis, loans except for certain real estate and guaranteed educational loans may be made up to $10,000 net of the borrower's shares, whenever capital is in excess of $3,000,000. The maximum limit for the net aggregate liability of any member as maker or otherwise is $20,000 net of the borrower's shares, for any credit union with a capital in excess of $3,000,000 (*New York Banking Law* S454).

Unsecured loans of federal credit unions are limited to $750 and individual loans cannot exceed 10 per cent of the credit union's unimpaired capital.[3]

Commercial Banks. The personal loan departments of all commercial banks, national and state, are governed by the state banking laws. Thus the loan limits and maximum charges are the same for the personal loan departments of both national and state banks.

The New York Banking Law[4] prescribes the maximum loan size and interest rates of personal loan departments of commercial banks as follows: Charges may be taken in advance, computed from the date of the loan to the date of the last installment, at a rate not greater than six dollars per annum discount per one hundred dollars of the face amount of the loan and the maximum size of the loan subject to these charges is $5,000.[5]

[3] Banks and Banking, Federal Credit Union Act, 12 U.S.C. S1761c.

[4] *New York Banking Law* S10 846, 1962.

[5] Banks are also permitted to offer revolving check credit plans subject to the same limit on loan sizes and a ceiling on rates of one per cent per month (which rate is approximately the same as the $6 discount rate mentioned here). Revolving check credit involves arranging for a credit line for a consumer (under written agreement) that can be increased from time to time by the cashing of checks and that automatically adds to the total amount of the loan.

APPENDIX B

Rate Ceilings and Loan Limits of the Consumer Finance Industry, by State, (1964)

State	1964 Rate Structure	Average Legal Rate on Loans of[a]			
		$100	$300	$500	$800
Alabama	3-2% @ $200 to $300; $1 per $5 of loans not exceeding $75	35.88	34.27		
Alaska	4-2½% @ $300, 2% @ $600 to $1,000, 5% on loans not exceeding $50; default fee of $3	48.09	47.96	44.31	39.54
Arizona	3-2% @ $300, 1% @ $600 to $1,000	36.08	36.01	33.63	29.77
California	2½-2% @ $200 (2% if security insured), 5-6% @ $500 to $5,000; no max. above $5,000	30.03	29.14	27.58	24.03
Colorado	3-1½% @ $300, 1% @ $500 to $1,500	36.08	36.01	32.46	27.22
Connecticut	$17-$9 a year per $100 @ $300 to $1,000 add-on; 12% a year after deferred maximum maturity	30.03	30.03	24.28	21.47
Delaware	6% a year discount; 2% service fee; 5% fine; various limitations; industrial law; loan size based on capital and surplus	15.72	15.65	15.68	15.67
Florida	3-2% @ $300 to $600; 10% a year 12 months after maturity	36.48	36.48	34.07	
Georgia	8% a year, to $2,500 discount for 18 months, add-on for longer maturities; fee of 8% of first $600 and 4% of excess	33.47	33.47	33.47	30.10

(continued)

State	1964 Rate Structure	Average Legal Rate on Loans of[a]			
		$100	$300	$500	$800
Hawaii	3½-2½% @ $100 to $300	42.62	36.61		
Idaho	3-2% @ $300, 1% @ $500 to $1,000	36.08	36.01	33.63	28.75
Illinois	3-2% @ $150, 1% @ $300 to $800	36.08	32.46	27.33	22.63
Indiana	3-2% @ $150, 1½% @ $300 to $1,000	36.46	32.93	28.85	25.50
Iowa	3-2% @ $150, 1½% @ $300 to $500	36.48	32.93	28.85	
Kansas	3-5/6% @ $300 to $2,100; 10% a year 6 months after maturity	36.08	36.01	30.96	24.91
Kentucky	3-2% @ $150, 1% $600 to $800; or add-on rates; $20 to $15 a year per $100 @ $150, $11 @ $600 to $800	35.07	30.91	29.17	26.53
Louisiana	3½-2½% @ $150 to $300; 8% a year 1 year after maturity	42.62	38.93		
Maine	3-2½% @ $150, 1½% @ $300 to $2,500; 25¢ minimum	36.08	34.20	30.47	26.71
Maryland	3% to $300	36.08	36.01		
Massachusetts	2½-2% @ $200, 1¾% @ $600, ¾% @ $1,000 to $3,000; 6% a year 1 year after maturity	30.03	29.14	27.58	26.14
Michigan	2½-1¼% @ $300 to $1,000	30.43	30.43	27.46	23.90
Minnesota	2¾-1½% @ $300 to $600	33.06	33.00	30.07	
Mississippi	Brokers' service charge and lender's interest not to exceed 2% per month add-on on loans of $100 or more, graduated scale for smaller loans; no maximum amount	41.64	41.70	41.72	41.71
Missouri	2.218% to $500; 8% a year on remainder	26.55	26.62	26.64	23.44
Montana	$20-$16 a year per $100 @ $300, $12 @ $500 to $1,000 add-on; special rate for loans up to $90	35.07		32.38	
Nebraska	2½-2% @ $300, 1½% @ $500, 1% @ $1,000 to $3,000	30.03	30.03	28.80	26.37

(continued)

State	1964 Rate Structure	Average Legal Rate on Loans of[a]			
		$100	$300	$500	$800
Nevada	9-8% a year @ $1,000 to $2,500 plus monthly fee of 1¢ per $1 to $200 and ½¢ per $1 from $200 to $400, all add-on	36.68		28.64	
New Hampshire	$16-$12 a year per $100 @ $600 to $1,500 add-on; 6% a year 6 months after maturity	28.19		28.31	
New Jersey	2½-½% @ $300 to $500	36.08	34.20	29.33	24.19
New Mexico	3-2½% @ $150, 1% @ $300 to $1,000; 10% a year 1 year after maturity and in certain other cases	36.08	34.20	29.33	24.19
New York	2½-2% @ $100, ¾% @ $300 to $800	30.03	27.10	23.13	18.93
North Carolina	$20-$18 a year per $100 @ $100, $15 @ $200 to $300, $6 @ $300 to $600 add-on; 6% a year 1 year after maturity; $1 per $5 of loans not exceeding $75	35.07		23.17	
North Dakota	2½-2% @ $250, 1¾% @ $500 to $750, 1½% @ $750 to $1,000	30.03	29.76	28.23	26.37
Ohio	$16-$9 a year per $100 @ $500, $7 @ $1,000 to $2,000 add-on; or equivalent simple interest rates	28.19		28.31	
Oklahoma	10% a year plus service charges not exceeding an initial 5% and monthly 2% but not more than $2, subject to various limitations to $300				
Oregon	3-2% @ $300, 1% @ $500 to $1,500	36.08	36.01	33.63	28.75
Pennsylvania	3-2% @ $150, 1% @ $300 to $600, 6% a year after 24 months	36.08	32.46	27.33	
Rhode Island	3% to $300				
South Carolina	Initial charge, 6% of cash advance plus 6% per annum to $200; $1.75 per month expense fee on loans $100 or over; 7% per annum on portion over $200; no maximum loan size				
South Dakota	3¾% @ $300 to $2,500; $2 minimum; 8% a year; 6 months after maturity	36.08	36.01	30.76	24.47

(continued)

State	1964 Rate Structure	Average Legal Rate on Loans of[a]			
		$100	$300	$500	$800
Tennessee	½% to $300; monthly fee not exceeding 1%	18.04	17.97		
Texas	$19-$16 a year per $100 @ $100, $13 @ $200, $11 @ $300, $9 @ $500, $7 @ $1,000 to $1,500 add-on; special rate for loans up to $100	33.26		24.91	
Utah	3-1% @ $300 to $600	36.68	36.48	31.73	
Vermont	2½-2¼% @ $125, 1% @ $300 to $600	30.43	29.21	25.69	
Virginia	2½-1½% @ $300 to $600; 6% a year after 23 months and in certain other areas	30.43	30.43	28.03	
Washington	3-1½% @ $300, 1% @ $500 to $1,000; $1 minimum	36.08	36.01	32.46	27.22
West Virginia	3-2% @ $200, 1½% @ $600 to $800; or add-on rates, $19-$16 a year per $100 @ $200, $12 @ $600 to $800				
Wisconsin	2½-2% @ $100, 1% @ $200 to $300	30.03	25.39		
Wyoming	3½-2½% @ $150; 1% @ $300 to $1,000; plus $1 fee on loans of $50 or less; $1 recording fee	42.03	38.40	32.13	26.02

[a] In all cases a 12-month, equal installment contract is assumed.

NOTE: Arkansas has no small loan law.

SOURCE: National Consumer Finance Association, *Consumer Finance Rate and Regulation Chart*, mimeo, 1964; Charles H. Gushee, Financial Publishing Company, in a mimeographed table of legal rates, supplied to the author on November 9, 1966.

APPENDIX C

Basic Statistical Data

In Table C-1 the following notations are used and are consistent with the notations used in the equations in Chapters 4-7. All data are for 1964 unless otherwise indicated.

X_1 = the loan limit (in hundreds of dollars).

X_2 = the legal rate, in "simple interest" per cent per annum, on loans of $100.

X_3 = the legal rate, in "simple interest" per cent per annum, on loans of $300.

X_4 = the legal rate, in "simple interest" per cent per annum, on loans of $500.

X_5 = the legal rate, in "simple interest" per cent per annum, on loans of $800.

X_6 = the average size of loan made (in dollars).

X_7 = the per capita income of the state (in hundreds of dollars).

X_8 = the average gross annual rate charged by all lenders in the state (in per cent). It is computed as the ratio of gross income to average dollar value of loans outstanding. Gross income here includes finance charges, recording fees, insurance and all other revenues associated with the regulated lending operations. Loans outstanding are net of unearned charges. The average loans outstanding are monthly averages where available; otherwise the averages of year-end 1963 and 1964 are used or the average of mid-year 1964 and mid-year 1965 where year-end figures were unavailable.

X_9 = the operating expenses (i.e., all expenses excluding only the interest paid and state and federal income taxes) as a percentage of average loans outstanding. Average loans outstanding are computed as in X_8.

X_{10} = the reserve for bad debts as a percentage of average loans outstanding in 1964. Average loans outstanding are computed as in X_8.

X_{11} = the number of finance companies' loan branches per 1,000 households.

X_{12} = the number of credit unions per 1,000 households.

X_{13} = the number of commercial bank branches per 1,000 households.

X_{14} = the number of finance company lenders per 1,000 households.

X_{15} = the average simple annual growth rate of the state's population over the 1960-64 period (in per cent).

X_{16} = the loans made per lender (in hundreds of thousands of dollars).

X_{17} = the number of loan branches per lender.

X_{18} = the loans made per loan branch (in hundreds of thousands of dollars).

X_{19} = the number of loans made per 1,000 households.

X_{20} = the dollar value of loans made per 1,000 households (in thousands of dollars).

X_{21} = the average net annual earnings of consumer finance companies as a percentage of their average loans outstanding. Net earnings are computed as total gross income (as in X_8) less all expenses, excluding income taxes (state and federal) and interest paid on borrowed funds. Average loans outstanding are computed as in X_8.

TABLE C-1
BASIC STATISTICAL DATA, 1964

State	X_1	X_2	X_3	X_4	X_5	X_6	X_7	X_8	X_9	X_{10}
Alabama[a]	3.00	35.88	34.27	NA	NA	82.12	15.38	40.68	32.18	3.90
Alaska[a]	10.00	48.09	47.96	44.31	39.54	NA	24.13	NA	NA	NA
Arizona	10.00	36.08	36.01	33.63	29.77	510.00	19.60	27.94	19.14	3.30
Arkansas	NA	NA	NA	NA	NA	NA	15.58	NA	NA	NA
California	50.00	30.03	29.14	27.58	24.03	627.14	26.56	22.75	14.33	2.50
Colorado	15.00	36.08	36.01	32.46	27.22	545.34	22.52	25.74	17.34	4.60
Connecticut[a]	10.00	30.03	30.03	24.58	21.47	605.78	27.91	22.21	11.81	2.60
Delaware	NA	15.72	15.65	15.68	15.67	NA	27.83	NA	NA	NA
Florida[a]	6.00	36.48	36.48	34.07	NA	416.00	19.57	29.05	18.95	3.30
Georgia[a]	25.00	33.47	33.47	33.47	30.10	327.15	17.55	30.72	20.50	NA
Hawaii[a]	3.00	42.62	36.61	NA	NA	NA	21.06	NA	NA	NA
Idaho[a]	10.00	36.08	36.01	33.63	28.75	516.50	18.19	26.76	16.46	1.70
Illinois[a]	8.00	36.08	32.46	27.33	22.63	471.26	26.10	24.37	15.47	2.90
Iowa[a]	5.00	36.48	32.93	28.85	NA	341.16	21.22	26.24	18.29	4.30
Kansas	21.00	36.08	36.01	30.96	24.91	696.76	20.41	21.18	12.48	2.50
Kentucky[a]	8.00	35.07	30.91	29.17	26.53	479.24	16.87	25.68	16.38	3.50
Louisiana	3.00	42.62	38.93	NA	NA	197.93	16.50	35.45	25.15	4.20
Maine	25.00	36.08	34.20	30.47	26.71	NA	18.69	NA	NA	NA
Maryland[a]	3.00	36.08	36.01	NA	NA	247.65	24.80	33.18	25.48	8.00
Massachusetts[a]	30.00	30.03	29.14	27.58	26.14	588.45	25.35	23.36	11.56	3.00
Michigan[a]	10.00	30.43	30.43	27.46	23.90	582.30	23.59	22.33	12.43	3.30
Minnesota[a]	6.00	33.06	33.00	30.07	NA	370.30	20.87	29.64	19.74	3.90
Mississippi	NA	41.64	41.70	41.72	41.71	NA	13.88	NA	NA	NA

(continued)

TABLE C-1 (continued)

State	X_1	X_2	X_3	X_4	X_5	X_6	X_7	X_8	X_9	X_{10}
Missouri	NA	26.55	26.62	26.64	23.44	NA	22.66	NA	NA	NA
Montana	10.00	35.07	NA	32.38	NA	568.00	20.04	25.28	16.58	NA
Nebraska[a]	30.00	30.03	30.03	28.80	26.37	577.02	21.44	21.23	13.36	NA
Nevada[a]	15.00	36.68	NA	28.64	NA	560.02	29.98	24.14	16.61	3.70
New Hampshire	15.00	28.19	NA	28.31	NA	632.46	21.37	25.91	17.11	1.80
New Jersey[a]	5.00	30.03	29.96	25.40	NA	NA	26.05	22.55	12.95	NA
New Mexico[a]	10.00	36.08	34.20	29.33	24.19	500.08	17.79	24.32	15.02	3.10
New York[a]	8.00	30.03	27.10	23.13	18.93	544.37	27.08	20.63	10.83	2.89
North Carolina[a]	6.00	35.07	NA	23.17	NA	NA	17.04	NA	NA	NA
North Dakota	10.00	30.03	29.76	28.23	26.37	461.60	18.94	25.00	NA	2.90
Ohio[a]	20.00	28.19	NA	28.31	NA	672.00	22.35	20.81	10.61	2.90
Oklahoma[a]	3.00	NA	NA	NA	NA	179.01	18.92	29.15	NA	NA
Oregon[a]	15.00	36.08	36.01	33.63	28.75	587.95	22.30	24.44	15.44	NA
Pennsylvania[a]	6.00	36.08	32.46	27.33	NA	NA	22.16	NA	NA	NA
Rhode Island[a]	3.00	NA	NA	NA	NA	NA	21.97	NA	NA	NA
South Carolina[a]	NA	NA	NA	NA	NA	211.75	14.87	32.35	23.75	3.80
South Dakota	25.00	36.08	36.01	30.76	24.47	450.31	18.55	NA	NA	NA
Tennessee	3.00	18.04	17.97	NA	NA	NA	16.78	NA	NA	NA
Texas	10.00	33.26	NA	24.91	NA	NA	19.04	NA	NA	NA
Utah[a]	6.00	36.68	36.48	31.73	NA	NA	19.35	NA	NA	NA
Vermont[a]	6.00	30.43	29.21	25.69	NA	431.87	19.42	23.13	13.43	3.50
Virginia[a]	6.00	30.43	30.43	28.03	NA	417.70	19.31	25.85	14.15	NA
Washington[a]	10.00	36.08	36.01	32.46	27.22	512.13	22.73	25.60	14.90	2.80
West Virginia[a]	8.00	NA	NA	NA	NA	447.30	17.81	28.55	15.25	3.00
Wisconsin[a]	3.00	30.03	25.39	NA	NA	203.00	20.98	27.10	NA	NA
Wyoming	10.00	42.03	38.40	32.13	26.02	NA	22.14	NA	NA	NA

(continued)

TABLE C-1 (continued)

State	X_{11}	X_{12}	X_{13}	X_{14}	X_{15}	X_{16}	X_{17}	X_{18}	X_{19}	X_{20}	X_{21}
Alabama[a]	0.49	0.34	0.43	0.22	1.10	332.00	2.25	148.00	891.50	73.20	8.50
Alaska[a]	0.20	0.48	0.81	0.06	2.20	NA	3.50	NA	NA	NA	NA
Arizona	0.54	NA	NA	0.14	4.00	1,106.00	3.78	292.00	311.72	159.00	8.80
Arkansas	NA	NA	NA	NA	1.80	NA	NA	NA	NA	NA	NA
California	0.28	0.30	0.46	0.06	3.20	3,093.00	5.13	925.00	271.68	170.00	8.52
Colorado	0.69	0.54	0.35	NA	2.20	NA	NA	288.00	366.29	199.70	8.40
Connecticut[a]	0.14	0.59	0.68	0.05	2.10	2,243.00	3.03	741.00	175.92	106.52	10.40
Delaware	NA	NA	NA	NA	2.40	NA	NA	NA	NA	NA	NA
Florida[a]	0.39	0.31	0.24	NA	3.00	NA	NA	316.00	292.66	121.76	10.10
Georgia[a]	0.92	0.32	0.51	0.38	1.90	850.00	2.44	348.00	974.25	318.73	10.20
Hawaii[a]	NA	NA	NA	NA	2.20	NA	NA	NA	NA	NA	NA
Idaho[a]	0.61	0.83	0.73	0.17	0.70	1,148.00	3.69	312.00	370.54	191.11	10.30
Illinois[a]	0.27	NA	NA	NA	1.00	NA	NA	381.00	216.86	102.20	8.90
Iowa[a]	0.37	NA	NA	0.15	0.00	384.00	2.48	155.00	162.52	57.16	8.00
Kansas	0.51	0.44	0.86	NA	0.50	NA	NA	419.00	305.60	212.80	8.70
Kentucky[a]	0.47	0.27	0.66	NA	0.90	NA	NA	433.00	427.84	205.00	9.30
Louisiana	0.66	0.46	0.48	NA	1.60	NA	NA	87.00	289.34	57.29	10.30
Maine	NA	NA	NA	NA	0.50	NA	NA	NA	NA	NA	9.60
Maryland[a]	0.38	0.21	0.57	0.10	2.40	833.00	3.83	218.00	331.47	82.11	7.70
Massachusetts[a]	0.21	NA	NA	0.06	0.70	2,033.00	3.86	526.00	190.46	112.07	11.80
Michigan[a]	0.27	0.51	0.51	0.06	0.90	2,442.00	4.20	582.00	268.73	1,035.60	9.90
Minnesota[a]	0.15	0.48	0.71	0.06	0.80	792,00	2.28	347.00	137.77	51.02	9.90
Mississippi	NA	NA	NA	NA	1.20	NA	NA	NA	NA	NA	NA
Missouri	0.46	0.43	0.47	0.15	0.80	1,222.00	3.17	386.00	281.47	177.47	7.90
Montana	0.26	0.66	0.61	0.04	0.90	1,755.00	5.91	299.00	136.76	77.68	8.70
Nebraska[a]	0.46	0.39	0.98	NA	0.90	NA	NA	343.00	270.43	156.04	7.87

(continued)

TABLE C-1 (continued)

State	X_{11}	X_{12}	X_{13}	X_{14}	X_{15}	X_{16}	X_{17}	X_{18}	X_{19}	X_{20}	X_{21}
Nevada[a]	0.40	0.55	0.64	0.15	8.20	1,348.00	3.68	502.00	358.21	200.61	7.53
New Hampshire	0.58	NA	NA	0.17	1.90	1,186.00	3.35	350.00	327.75	207.29	8.80
New Jersey[a]	0.15	NA	NA	0.04	2.10	NA	4.37	NA	NA	NA	9.60
New Mexico[a]	0.76	0.43	0.53	NA	1.50	NA	NA	363.00	559.71	274.82	9.30
New York[a]	0.09	NA	NA	0.01	1.40	9,143.00	8.81	1,038.00	174.50	94.99	9.80
North Carolina[a]	NA	0.21	0.67	NA	1.40	NA	NA	NA	NA	NA	NA
North Dakota	0.35	NA	NA	0.12	0.60	781.00	2.82	277.00	203.20	97.85	NA
Ohio[a]	0.45	0.42	0.46	NA	1.00	NA	NA	457.00	303.41	204.06	10.20
Oregon[a]	0.31	NA	NA	0.10	1.20	140.00	3.43	41.00	71.17	12.73	3.30
Oklahoma[a]	0.39	0.39	0.51	NA	1.40	NA	NA	368.00	224.12	131.80	9.00
Pennsylvania[a]	0.29	NA	NA	0.07	0.30	NA	4.25	NA	NA	NA	NA
Rhode Island[a]	NA	NA	NA	NA	0.70	NA	NA	NA	NA	NA	NA
South Carolina[a]	0.99	0.20	0.57	NA	1.20	NA	NA	248.00	1,161.52	245.95	8.60
South Dakota	0.52	0.48	0.22	NA	0.60	NA	NA	259.00	297.27	133.80	NA
Tennessee	0.66	NA	NA	0.19	1.40	NA	3.58	NA	NA	NA	NA
Texas	NA	NA	NA	NA	1.80	NA	NA	NA	NA	NA	NA
Utah[a]	0.58	NA	NA	NA	2.00	NA	NA	NA	NA	NA	NA
Vermont[a]	0.26	0.63	0.93	0.09	0.40	1,272.00	2.90	439.00	261.38	112.58	9.70
Virginia[a]	0.25	0.25	0.66	0.05	2.20	3,041.00	4.51	662.00	396.71	165.63	11.70
Washington[a]	0.23	0.36	0.53	0.03	0.90	3,388.00	7.59	447.00	201.09	102.97	10.70
West Virginia[a]	0.42	NA	NA	0.14	NA	1,172.00	2.95	396.00	371.60	166.22	13.30
Wisconsin[a]	0.21	0.63	0.61	NA	0.90	NA	NA	53.00	53.31	10.84	4.90
Wyoming	NA	NA	NA	NA	0.60	NA	NA	NA	NA	NA	NA

[a] C & A states.

Source: Computed from Reports of the State Supervisors.

Note: Indiana and Mississippi were excluded from all computations because of inadequacies of data on their operations.

NA = not applicable.

APPENDIX D

Percentage Distribution of Number of Loans Made, New York State, 1936-65

Year	$100 or Less	$100.01 to $200	$200.01 to $300	$300.01 to $400	$400.01 to $500	$500.01 to $600	$600.01 to $700	$700.01 to $800	Average All Loa (dollar
1936	40.0	33.2	26.8	NA	NA	NA	NA	NA	157.6
1937	39.5	32.2	28.3	NA	NA	NA	NA	NA	159.2
1938	40.2	32.1	27.7	NA	NA	NA	NA	NA	156.1
1939	41.5	30.8	27.7	NA	NA	NA	NA	NA	154.5
1940	40.0	30.8	29.2	NA	NA	NA	NA	NA	157.9
1941	34.0	33.7	32.3	NA	NA	NA	NA	NA	165.5
1942	38.4	30.1	31.5	NA	NA	NA	NA	NA	162.7
1943	38.0	31.2	30.8	NA	NA	NA	NA	NA	163.7
1944	33.8	32.5	33.7	NA	NA	NA	NA	NA	173.2
1945	29.0	32.5	38.5	NA	NA	NA	NA	NA	184.8
1946	26.2	31.1	42.7	NA	NA	NA	NA	NA	193.8
1947	22.4	29.1	48.3	NA	NA	NA	NA	NA	204.3
1948	19.5	27.7	52.8	NA	NA	NA	NA	NA	211.3
1949	15.5	24.5	40.4	9.1	10.5	NA	NA	NA	245.0
1950	13.0	22.4	21.8	19.1	23.7	NA	NA	NA	277.0
1951	11.6	20.8	20.4	17.5	29.7	NA	NA	NA	294.0
1952	9.6	19.4	19.4	17.3	34.3	NA	NA	NA	309.0
1953	8.6	17.8	17.6	16.7	39.3	NA	NA	NA	323.0
1954	8.3	17.0	16.8	16.7	41.2	NA	NA	NA	328.0
1955	7.4	16.2	16.4	16.3	43.7	NA	NA	NA	336.0
1956	6.4	14.5	15.5	15.7	47.9	NA	NA	NA	350.0
1957	5.9	13.9	14.7	14.8	50.7	NA	NA	NA	359.0
1958	5.5	13.2	13.9	14.1	53.3	NA	NA	NA	367.0
1959	4.6	12.5	13.4	14.0	55.5	NA	NA	NA	375.0
1960	3.6	10.5	11.6	11.9	31.0	9.2	7.1	15.1	450.0
1961	3.3	10.2	11.6	11.4	9.2	14.5	11.3	28.5	498.0
1962	3.0	9.9	11.0	11.4	9.2	12.4	10.8	32.3	520.0
1963	2.8	9.5	10.7	11.0	9.1	11.2	10.2	35.5	535.0
1964	2.4	8.9	10.3	10.6	8.9	10.4	9.9	38.6	544.0
1965	2.1	8.0	9.8	10.3	8.8	10.4	9.5	41.5	555.0

Source: New York State Consumer Finance Association. *Statistical Information on All Licensed Lenders*, mimeo, 1965.
NA = not available.

APPENDIX E

Number of Branches Per Lender, New York State, 1932-65

Year	Number of Lenders	Number of Branches	Number of Branches per Lender
1932	29	78	2.7
1933	42	143	3.4
1934	51	186	3.6
1935	59	205	3.5
1936	61	237	3.9
1937	64	265	4.1
1938	61	269	4.4
1939	67	288	4.3
1940	69	308	4.5
1941	75	317	4.2
1942	66	298	4.5
1943	57	268	4.7
1944	58	269	4.6
1945	57	270	4.7
1946	57	282	4.9
1947	60	286	4.8
1948	61	289	4.7
1949	61	296	4.9
1950	62	314	4.9
1951	60	328	5.1
1952	60	335	5.5
1953	67	356	5.6
1954	73	385	5.3
1955	74	408	5.3
1956	74	437	5.5
1957	64	441	5.9
1958	64	450	6.9
1959	64	465	7.0
1960	61	470	7.2
1961	59	475	7.7
1962	59	485	8.1
1963	56	494	8.1
1964	57	502	8.8
1965	54	511	9.5

Source: New York State Consumer Finance Association, *Statistical Information on All Licensed Lenders in New York State*, mimeo, 1965.

APPENDIX F

Changes in the Number and Amount of Loans Made in New York State, 1936-65

Year	Number of Loans Made During Year	Increase Over Previous Year (per cent)	Amount of Loans During Year (thousands of dollars)	Increase Over Previous Year (per cent)
1936	533,151	–	84,052.2	–
1937	649,793	2.2	103,448.3	23.1
1938	660,217	1.6	103,075.6	–.4
1939	843,045	27.7	130,306.5	26.4
1940	930,597	10.4	146,954.7	12.8
1941	899,588	–3.3	148,920.3	1.3
1942	693,798	–22.9	112,906.8	–24.2
1943	626,916	–9.6	102,677.5	–9.1
1944	626,722	–(0.0)	108,547.5	5.7
1945	632,987	1.0	116,995.6	7.8
1946	750,093	18.5	145,432.0	24.3
1947	813,906	8.5	166,321.0	14.4
1948	820,476	0.8	173,443.0	4.3
1949[a]	889,538	8.4	218,122.0	25.8
1950	879,146	–1.2	243,539.0	11.7
1951	961,997	9.4	283,640.0	16.5
1952	1,011,090	5.1	313,076.0	10.4
1953	1,016,481	0.0	328,738.0	5.0
1954	1,044,434	2.7	343,119.0	4.4
1955	1,083,895	3.6	365,172.0	6.4
1956	1,162,550	7.3	407,032.0	11.5
1957	1,156,585	0.0	416,090.0	2.2
1958	1,095,929	–5.5	402,737.0	–3.2
1959	1,101,354	0.0	413,069.0	2.6
1960[a]	1,117,417	1.5	502,850.0	21.7
1961	919,198	–22.7	457,782.0	–9.8
1962	960,718	4.5	499,579.0	9.1
1963	945,940	–1.5	505,634.0	1.2
1964	957,339	1.2	521,143.9	3.1
1965	975,803	1.9	541,784.8	4.0

[a] Years in which there were loan ceiling changes.

SOURCE: Computed from New York State Consumer Finance Association, *Statistical Information on All Licensed Lenders*, mimeo, 1965.

Bei Fragen zur Produktsicherheit wenden Sie sich bitte an:
If you have any questions regarding product safety,
please contact:

Walter de Gruyter GmbH
Genthiner Straße 13
10785 Berlin
productsafety@degruyterbrill.com